CHRISTIAN LIBERTY PRESS
502 West Euclid Avenue, Arlington Heights, Illinois 60004

2017 Printing

For sources and permissions, see page 227.

Compiled and edited by Elizabeth Kearney
Copyedited by Diane C. Olson
Cover art and text illustrations by David Miles
Design and layout by Bob Fine

ISBN 978-1-932971-67-5 (print)
ISBN 978-1-935796-80-0 (eBook PDF)

A publication of
CHRISTIAN LIBERTY PRESS
502 W. Euclid Avenue
Arlington Heights, IL 60004
www.christianlibertypress.com

Printed in the United States of America

Contents

Unit 6: Important People—Turn of the Century

Unit 7: The Life of the Cowboy

Unit 8: Tales of the Rails

Unit 9: The Twentieth Century

Introduction

Building a New Nation is an exciting collection of reading selections that picks up where *Finding a New Land*, Christian Liberty Press's fourth grade reader, leaves off. Children will experience important historical events from America's westward expansion in the nineteenth century until well into the twentieth century. Readers will learn about important people such as Davy Crockett, Clara Barton, Abraham Lincoln, Robert E. Lee, Adoniram Judson, and Booker T. Washington.

This colorful reader is designed to provide children with a better understanding of the growth of the nation through historical fiction, true stories, biographical accounts, American folk tales, and poetry. In addition to enjoyable and uplifting reading selections, this book provides students with vocabulary definitions, comprehension questions, and additional activities at the end of most selections.

Parents and teachers will be able to use the textbook questions to assess their students' reading comprehension. Along with this reader, we have developed an accompanying teacher's manual to help instructors by providing answers to the reader's questions. In addition, there is a *Student Exercises* workbook that allows students to take a deeper look at certain reading selections. Finally, we have created a set of tests to help parents and teachers further evaluate their students' understanding of the stories.

We are confident that students will find this well-illustrated book to be both enjoyable and informative. More importantly, we trust that it will help them to gain a better understanding of how the events and personalities during the development of America affected the lives of young people many years ago.

May God bless you and your students in the use of *Building a New Nation*.

The Publishers
Arlington Heights, Illinois

Unit 1
American Tales

Johnny Appleseed:
The Life of John Chapman

Carolyn Bailey

John Chapman was a real farmer who was born in Massachusetts in the late 1700s. Read to find out why his story has been handed down from generation to generation.

"'We can hear him read now, just as he did that summer day, when we were busy quilting upstairs, and he lay near the door, his voice rising ***denunciatory*** *and thrilling—strong and loud as the roar of wind and waves, then soft and soothing as the balmy airs that quivered the morning-glory leaves about his gray beard. His was a strange eloquence at times, and he was undoubtedly a man of genius,' reported a lady who knew him in his later years."*

There was once a farmer who had worked in the fields all his life. Every year he had plowed and planted and harvested, and no one else had raised such fine crops as he. It seemed as if he needed to only touch the corn to have it yellow and ripen upon the ear, or lay his hand upon the rough bark of a tree to be sure that the blossoms would show and the branches hang low with fruit.

After years and years, the farmer grew to be an old man. His hair and beard became as white as the blossoms on the pear trees, and his back was bent and crooked because he had worked so hard. He could only sit in the sunshine and watch someone else plowing and planting where he wanted so much to plow and plant. And he felt very unhappy because he wished to do something great for other people, and he was not able, for he was poor.

One morning he got down his **stout** cane from the chimney corner, and he slung an empty bag over his crooked old shoulders, and he started out into the world because he had thought of a good deed that even an old man could do.

Over the meadows and through the lanes he traveled, stopping to speak to the little wild mice or the crickets or the chipmunks, who knew him—all of them—and were never afraid when he went by. At every farmhouse he rested and knocked at the door and asked for—what do you think?—just a few apples! And the farmers had so many apples that they were glad to give some of them away, and the old man's bag was soon full to the very **brim**.

On and on he went, until he left the houses far behind and took his way through the deep woods. At night he slept upon a bed of moss out under the stars, with the prairie dogs barking in his ears and the owls hooting in the tops of the trees; and in the morning he started on his way again.

When he was hungry, he ate of the berries that grew in the woods, but not one of his apples—oh, no! Sometimes an Indian met him, and they walked along together; and so, at last, the old man came to a place where there were wide fields, but no one to plant them, for there were no farms.

Then he sat down and took out his jack-knife, and began carefully cutting the core from every apple in his bag. With his stout cane he **bored** deep holes in the earth, and in every hole he dropped an apple core, to sleep there in the rain and the sun. And when his bag was emptied, he hurried on to a town where he could ask for more apples.

Soon the farmers came to know him, and they called him old Apple-seed John. They gave him their very best apples for seed—the Pound Sweets, and the Sheep's Noses, and the Pippins,

and the Seek-no-Farthers. They saved clippings from the pear trees, and the plum trees, and the peach trees for him; and they gave him the corner of the **settle** that was nearest the fire when he stopped with them for a night.

Such wonderful stories as he told the children of the things he had seen in his travels—the Indians with their bright blankets and feathers, the wolves who came out of the wood at night to look at him with their glaring eyes, the deer who ran across his path, and the shy little hares. He also shared the Gospel with young and old alike. No one ever wished Apple-seed John to travel on the next morning, but he would never stay. With his bag over his shoulder, his clippings under his arm, and his trusty cane in his hand, he hurried on to plant young orchards by every river and in every lonely pasture. Soon the apple seeds that had been asleep when Apple-seed John had dropped them into the earth awoke and arose, and sent out green shoots, and began to be trees. Higher and higher they grew, until, in the wind and the sun, they covered the ground with blossoms, and then with ripe fruit, so that the entire empty places in the country were full of **orchards**.

After a while old Apple-seed John went to live with the angels, but no one ever forgot him; and the children who knew him, when they had grown to be grandfathers themselves, would sit out under the trees and say to each other: "This orchard was planted by Apple-seed John."

Vocabulary

denunciatory: accusing or condemning

stout: sturdy; strong

brim: the edge of the bag

bored: dug

settle: bench

orchard: a planting of many fruit trees

Comprehension Questions

1. Why did John Chapman decide to travel and plant orchards?
2. Here are some quotes that you might relate to John Chapman's life. Choose one and explain how it relates.

    Happiness is a by-product of an effort to make someone else happy. ~Gretta Brooker Palmer

    Pleasure is spread through the earth in stray gifts to be claimed by whoever shall find. ~William Wordsworth, 1806

    He is rich or poor according to what he is, not according to what he has. ~Henry Ward Beecher

3. John Chapman was a real person, but the legend of Johnny Appleseed, which contains some truths and some exaggerations, has been handed down from generation to generation. Why do you think the legend of Johnny Appleseed became so popular?

Extension Activity

Imagine the government has appointed you *to create a holiday named "John Chapman Day." Write a short plan for such a holiday. Why should people celebrate this day? What should they do to commemorate or celebrate?*

Round River

James MacGillivray

The following story is called a tall tale. Tall tales are humorous stories that contain unbelievable events. This tall tale is about Paul Bunyan, an imaginary American **lumberjack**. *It is told from the point of view of a fellow lumberjack on Paul Bunyan's crew.*

What! You never heard of the Round River drive? Don't suppose you ever read about Paul Bunyan, neither? And you call yourselves lumberjacks?

Why, back in Michigan, that's the one thing they asked you, and if you hadn't at least "**swamped**" for Paul you didn't get no job—not in no real lumber camp, anyway. You Idaho yaps may know how to ranch all right, but it's Maine or Michigan where they learn to do real **drivin'**—cept' Canada, of course.

You see, back in those days the government didn't care nothin' about the **timber**. It was there for the takin'. The first thing you did was find yourself a good runnin' stream. Then you just pile the logs up right next to it. Come springtime, you tumble the logs into the river and float 'em down to the **mill** fer sellin'. You was bound to strike either Lake Huron or Michigan, and it made no difference which, 'cause logs were the same price whichever, and there was always mills at the mouth of the stream to saw 'em into boards.

So Paul, he found himself the Round River drive—course he didn't know it was called the Round River then. He gets the bunch together, and a fine layout he had. There was me, Dutch Jake, Fred Klinard, and Pat O'Brien—"P-O-B"—and Saginaw

Joe, the McDonalds—Angus, Roy, Archie, Black Jack, Big Jack, and more. There was 300 men all told.

Canada Bill, he was the cook. He had two helpers who would skate round our gigantic stove with hams tied to their feet, greasin' the lid for the hotcakes. It went fine for a while till one morning "Squint-Eyed" Martin, the chore boy, mistook the gunpowder can for bakin' powder. The helpers had just done a double figure eight when Joe **commences** to flap on the batter. Good thing the explosion went upward so it saved the stove. But we never did find those helpers....

We'd placed our camp on the river's bank, and we commenced to cut down as many of them trees as was humanly possible. Of course, we had the help of Babe, Paul's blue ox, too.

We'd shoot for the timber on all four sides. One day we comes across some deer. "Forty-Four" Jones was buildin' the slide that rolled the logs into the stream, and he liked **game**. He didn't saynothin', but I knowed he had an idea. Sure enough, Jones gets up early next mornin' and he caught the deer comin' down to drink, and he starts the logs comin' down that slide and kills more than 200 of 'em. We had venison steak all winter, which went well with the pea soup.

What pea soup? Well, you see, we'd brought in a whole wagon load of peas, and the wagon broke and dumped the whole mess over into some nearby springs. The driver came in sorryful like, expectin' Paul to fire him right then and there. But Canada Bill, he says to Bunyan, "It's all right, Paul, them is hot springs." So he puts some pepper, salt, and a big hunk of pork in the springs, and we had pea soup to last us the whole job.

That Round River ox-team was the biggest ever heard of, I guess. They weighed 4,800 pounds. The barn boss made them a buckskin **harness** from the hides of the deer we'd killed, and the bull cook used them haulin' dead timber to camp for wood supply. But that harness sure upset them oxen when it got wet. You know how buckskin will stretch?

It was rainin' one mornin' when the bull cook went for wood. He put the strap on a nice sized log and started for camp. The oxen pulled all right, but that harness got to stretchin', and when the bull cook gets into camp, why the log wasn't there at all. He looks back, and there was the strap of that harness, stretched out in long lines disappearin' 'round the bend of the road, 'most as far as he could see. He's mad and disgusted like, and he jerks the harness off and throws the strap over a stump. Pretty soon the rain clears up. The sun come out, dryin' up that harness, and when the bull cook comes out from dinner, there's his log, hauled right into camp.

They was big trees that Bunyan lumbered that winter, and one of them pretty near made trouble. They used to keep a competition board hung in the **commissary**, showin' what each gang sawed for the week, and that's how it happened.

Dutch Jake and me had picked out the biggest tree we could find, and we'd put in three days cuttin' with our big saw. We was gettin' along fine on the fourth day when lunch time comes, and we thought we'd best get on the sunny side to eat. So we grabs our **grub can** and starts around that tree. We hadn't gone far when we heard a noise. There they were—Bill Carter and Sailor Jack sawin' at the same tree! It looked like a fight at first, but we **compromised**, meetin' each other at the heart on the seventh day. They'd hacked her to fall to the north, and we'd hacked her to fall to the south, and there that tree stood for a month or more, clean sawed through, but not knowin' which way to drop 'til a wind storm came along and blowed her over.

You should have seen the big men that Bunyan put on the landin' that spring when it was time to roll them logs into the river. All six-footers, and 200 pounds weight. Nothin' else would do, and the fellows that didn't come up to the regulations was tailed off to do other smaller jobs.

The river was runnin' high, and Bunyan was sure that we would soon hit either the "Sable" or Muskegon River, and he cared not which, fer logs would get the same price just about anywhere. We run on the river for two weeks, makin' about a mile a day when we struck a deserted camp that had been a lumberin' camp that must have been almost as large as Bunyan's from the signs on the banks. This was **peculiar**, for we didn't know of another lumber camp so nearby.

We drove along for another two weeks and hits another lumber camp, deserted like the last one, and Paul begins to get mighty upset, for he sees the price of logs fallin' with all this lumberin' on the one stream.

Well, we sacked and pulled them logs for three weeks more, and blamed if we didn't strike another camp. Then Bunyan gets wild! "Boys," he says, "if we strike any more of them camps, logs won't be worth thirty cents a thousand, and I won't be able to pay you off. Let's camp and talk it over," he says.

So we hits for the deserted shacks, and turnin' a corner, who was there? Those two helpers that had been blown up months ago, and at their feet was the hams! Then we knowed it was Round River, and we'd passed our own camp three times.

Did we ever locate the camp again? Well, some years afterwards, Tom Mellin and I runs a line west and we runs into the old camp one last time. But the stream had gone dry, and a fire had run through that country makin' an awful slashin', and those Round River logs was nothin' more than charcoal.

Vocabulary

lumberjack: a person who cut trees down for lumber

swamped: cleared small trees and shrubs away to make way for a road

drivin': a way of moving logs using a river's current to move them downstream to sawmills

timber: trees that have been cut down

mill: a building used for sawing logs

commences: begins; starts

game: meat from a hunted animal; in this case, deer

harness: the straps and fastenings by which an animal pulls a load

commissary: a store that provides food and supplies to workers

grub can: a can used to hold a worker's lunch

compromised: reached an agreement

peculiar: strange

Comprehension Questions

1. In your own words, explain what happened to the cook's assistants.
2. In your own words, explain how the men came to have pea soup.
3. Why did Paul Bunyan get upset when he thought he saw other lumbering camps?
4. Explain why the men kept coming across their own lumber camp.
5. This tall tale attempts to be humorous. What do you think was the most humorous part of the story?

Extension Activity

Imagine what would happen if Johnny Appleseed met Paul Bunyan. Write your own tall tale. Use the story planning sheet on page 1 of the Student Exercises *booklet.*

The Girl Who Owned a Bear

L. Frank Baum

L. Frank Baum wrote many humorous fairy tales. This one tells of some magical happenings with a little girl named Jane Gladys.

Mamma had gone downtown to shop. She had asked Nora to look after Jane Gladys, and Nora promised she would. But it was her afternoon for polishing the silver, so she stayed in the pantry and left Jane Gladys to amuse herself alone in the big sitting room upstairs.

The little girl did not mind being alone, for she was working on her first piece of embroidery—a sofa pillow for Papa's birthday present. So she crept into the big bay window and curled herself up on the broad sill while she bent her brown head over her work.

Soon the door opened and closed again, quietly. Jane Gladys thought it was Nora, so she didn't look up until she had taken a couple more stitches on a **forget-me-not**. Then she raised her eyes and was astonished to find a strange man in the middle of the room, who looked at her **earnestly**.

He was short and fat, and seemed to be breathing heavily from his climb up the stairs. He held a worn silk hat in one hand, and underneath his other elbow was tucked a good-sized book. He was dressed in a black suit that looked old and rather shabby, and his head was bald upon the top.

"Excuse me," he said, while the child gazed at him in solemn surprise. "Are you Jane Gladys Brown?"

"Yes, sir," she answered.

"Very good; very good, indeed!" he remarked, with a odd sort of smile. "I've had quite a hunt to find you, but I've succeeded at last."

"How did you get in?" inquired Jane Gladys, with a growing distrust of her visitor.

"That is a secret," he said mysteriously.

This was enough to put the girl on her guard. She looked at the man, and the man looked at her, and both looks were **grave** and somewhat anxious.

"What do you want?" she asked, straightening herself up with a dignified **air**.

"Ah!—now we are coming to business," said the man briskly. "I'm going to be quite frank with you. To begin with, your father has abused me in a most ungentlemanly manner."

Jane Gladys got off the window sill and pointed her small finger at the door.

"Leave this room 'meejitly!" she cried, her voice trembling with **indignation**. "My papa is the best man in the world. He never 'bused anybody!"

"Allow me to explain, please," said the visitor, without paying any attention to her request to go away. "Your father may be very kind to you, for you are his little girl, you know. But when he's downtown in his office he's inclined to be rather severe, especially on **book agents**. Now, I called on him the other day and asked him to buy the *Complete Works of Peter Smith*, and what do you suppose he did?"

She said nothing.

"Why," continued the man, with growing excitement, "he ordered me from his office and had me put out of the building by the janitor! What do you think of such treatment as that from the 'best papa in the world,' eh?"

"I think he was quite right," said Jane Gladys.

"Oh, you do? Well," said the man, "I resolved to be revenged for the insult. So, as your father is big and strong and a dangerous man, I have decided to be revenged upon his little girl."

Jane Gladys shivered.

"What are you going to do?" she asked.

"I'm going to present you with this book," he answered, taking it from under his arm. Then he sat down on the edge of a chair, placed his hat on the rug, and drew a fountain pen from his vest pocket.

"I'll write your name in it," said he. "How do you spell Gladys?"

"G-l-a-d-y-s," she replied.

"Thank you. Now this," he continued, rising and handing her the book with a bow, "is my revenge for your father's treatment of me. Perhaps he'll be sorry he didn't buy the *Complete Works of Peter Smith*. Good-bye, my dear."

He walked to the door, gave her another bow, and left the room; and Jane Gladys could see that he was laughing to himself as if very much amused.

When the door had closed behind the odd little man, the child sat down in the window again and glanced at the book. It had a red and yellow cover, and the word "Thingamajigs" was across the front in big letters.

Then she opened it, curiously, and saw her name written in black letters upon the first white **leaf**.

"He was a funny little man," she said to herself thoughtfully.

She turned the next leaf and saw a big picture of a clown, dressed in green and red and yellow, and having a very white face with three-cornered spots of red on each cheek and over the eyes. While she looked at this, the book trembled in her hands, the leaf crackled and creaked, and suddenly the clown jumped out of it and stood upon the floor beside her, becoming instantly as big as any ordinary clown.

After stretching his arms and legs and yawning in a rather impolite manner, he gave a silly chuckle and said, "This is better! You don't know how cramped one gets, standing so long upon a page of flat paper."

Perhaps you can imagine how startled Jane Gladys was, and how she stared at the clown who had just leaped out of the book.

"You didn't expect anything of this sort, did you?" he asked, leering at her in clown fashion. Then he turned around to take a look at the room, and Jane Gladys laughed in spite of her astonishment.

"What amuses you?" demanded the clown.

"Why, the back of you is all white!" cried the girl. "You're only a clown in front of you."

"Quite likely," he returned, in an annoyed tone. "The artist made a front view of me. He wasn't expected to make the back of me, for that was against the page of the book."

"But it makes you look so funny!" said Jane Gladys, laughing until her eyes were moist with tears.

The clown looked sulky and sat down upon a chair so she couldn't see his back.

"I'm not the only thing in the book," he remarked crossly.

This reminded her to turn another page, and she had scarcely noted that it contained the picture of a monkey when the animal sprang from the book with a great crumpling of paper and landed upon the window seat beside her.

"He-he-he-he-he!" chattered the creature, springing to the girl's shoulder and then to the center table. "This is great fun! Now I can be a real monkey instead of a picture of one."

"Real monkeys can't talk," said Jane Gladys **reprovingly**.

"How do you know? Have you ever been one yourself?" inquired the animal; and then he laughed loudly, and the clown laughed, too, as if he enjoyed the remark.

The girl was quite **bewildered** by this time. She thoughtlessly turned another leaf, and before she had time to look twice a gray donkey leaped from the book and stumbled from the window seat to the floor with a great clatter.

"You're clumsy enough, I'm sure!" said the child indignantly, for the beast had nearly run into her.

"Clumsy! And why not?" demanded the donkey, with angry voice. "If the fool artist had drawn you out of perspective, as he did me, I guess you'd be clumsy yourself."

"What's wrong with you?" asked Jane Gladys.

"My front and rear legs on the left side are nearly six inches too short; that's what's the matter! If that artist didn't know how to draw properly, why did he try to make a donkey at all?"

"I don't know," replied the child, seeing an answer was expected.

"I can hardly stand up," grumbled the donkey, "and the least little thing will topple me over."

"Don't mind that," said the monkey, making a spring at the chandelier and swinging from it by his tail until Jane Gladys feared he would knock all the **globes** off. "The same artist has made my ears as big as that clown's, and everyone knows a monkey hasn't any ears to speak of—much less to draw."

"He should be **prosecuted**," remarked the clown gloomily. "I haven't any back."

Jane Gladys looked from one to the other with a puzzled expression upon her sweet face, and turned another page of the book.

Swift as a flash there sprang over her shoulder a **tawny**, spotted leopard, which landed upon the back of a big leather armchair and turned upon the others with a fierce movement.

The monkey climbed to the top of the chandelier and chattered with fright. The donkey tried to run and straightway tipped over on his left side. The clown grew paler than ever, but he sat still in his chair and gave a low whistle of surprise.

The leopard crouched upon the back of the chair, lashed his tail from side to side, and glared at all of them, by turns, including Jane Gladys.

"Which of us are you going to attack first?" asked the donkey, trying hard to get upon his feet again.

"I can't attack any of you," snarled the leopard. "The artist made my mouth shut, so I haven't any teeth; and he forgot to make my claws. But I'm a frightful-looking creature, nevertheless; am I not?"

"Oh, yes," said the clown indifferently. "I suppose you're frightful looking enough. But if you have no teeth nor claws we don't mind your looks at all."

This so annoyed the leopard that he growled horribly, and the monkey laughed at him.

Just then the book slipped from the girl's lap, and as she made a movement to catch it one of the pages near the back opened wide. She caught a glimpse of a fierce grizzly bear looking at her from the page, and quickly threw the book from her. It fell with a crash in the middle of the room, but beside it stood the great grizzly, who had wrenched himself from the page before the book closed.

"Now," cried the leopard from his perch, "you'd better look out for yourselves! You can't laugh at him as you did at me. The bear has both claws and teeth."

"Indeed I have," said the bear in a low, deep, growling voice. "And I know how to use them, too. If you read in that book you'll find I'm described as a horrible, cruel, and **remorseless** grizzly, whose only business in life is to eat up little girls—shoes, dresses, ribbons, and all! And then, the author says, I smack my lips and glory in my wickedness."

"That's awful!" said the donkey, sitting upon his haunches and shaking his head sadly. "What do you suppose possessed the author to make you so hungry for girls? Do you eat animals, also?"

"The author does not mention my eating anything but little girls," replied the bear.

"Very good," remarked the clown, drawing a long breath of relief. "You may begin eating Jane Gladys as soon as you wish. She laughed because I had no back."

"And she laughed because my legs are out of perspective," brayed the donkey.

"But you also deserve to be eaten," screamed the leopard from the back of the leather chair, "for you laughed and poked fun at me because I had no claws nor teeth! Don't you suppose, Mr. Grizzly, you could manage to eat a clown, a donkey, and a monkey after you finish the girl?"

"Perhaps so, and a leopard into the bargain," growled the bear. "It will depend on how hungry I am. But I must begin on the little girl first because the author says I prefer girls to anything."

Jane Gladys was much frightened on hearing this conversation, and she began to realize what the man meant when he said he gave her the book to be revenged. Surely Papa would be sorry he hadn't bought the *Complete Works of Peter Smith* when he came home and found his little girl eaten up by a grizzly bear—shoes, dress, ribbons, and all!

The bear stood up and balanced himself on his rear legs.

"This is the way I look in the book," he said. "Now watch me eat the little girl."

He advanced slowly toward Jane Gladys; and the monkey, the leopard, the donkey, and the clown all stood around in a circle and watched the bear with much interest.

But before the grizzly reached her, the child had a sudden thought, and cried out, "Stop! You mustn't eat me. It would be wrong."

"Why?" asked the bear, in surprise.

"Because I own you. You're my private property," she answered.

"I don't see how you make that out," said the bear, in a disappointed tone.

"Why, the book was given to me; my name's on the front leaf. And you belong, by rights, in the book. So you mustn't dare to eat your owner!"

The grizzly hesitated.

"Can any of you read?" he asked.

"I can," said the clown.

"Then see if she speaks the truth. Is her name really in the book?"

The clown picked it up and looked at the name.

"It is," said he. "'Jane Gladys Brown,' and written quite plainly in big letters."

The bear sighed.

"Then, of course, I can't eat her," he decided. "That author is as disappointing as most authors are."

"But he's not as bad as the artist," exclaimed the donkey, who was still trying to stand up straight.

"The fault lies with yourselves," said Jane Gladys severely. "Why didn't you stay in the book, where you were put?"

The animals looked at each other in a foolish way, and the clown blushed under his white paint.

"Really..." began the bear, and then he stopped short.

The doorbell rang loudly.

"It's Mamma!" cried Jane Gladys, springing to her feet. "She's come home at last. Now, you stupid creatures..."

But she was interrupted by them all making a rush for the book. There was a swish and a whirr and a rustling of leaves, and an instant later the book lay upon the floor looking just like any other book, while Jane Gladys's strange companions had all disappeared.

Vocabulary

forget-me-not: a small blue or white flower

earnestly: thoughtfully

grave: serious

air: appearance

indignation: anger, caused by something unfair

book agents: buyers and sellers of books

leaf: page

reprovingly: with disapproval or rebuke

bewildered: confused

globes: round pieces of the chandelier

prosecuted: arrested

tawny: a brownish-orange color

remorseless: without feelings of guilt

Comprehension Questions

1. Why was the little man upset with Jane Gladys's father?
2. What was the first creature to come alive from the book? Why did Jane Gladys laugh at this creature?
3. How did Jane Gladys outwit the bear?
4. Why did the creatures go back into the book?
5. The author attempted to make this tale humorous. What part did you find most humorous?

Extension Activity

Many fairy tales have common elements. Fill out the Fairy Tale Analysis sheet on page 2 of the Student Exercises *booklet to further analyze "The Girl Who Owned a Bear."*

The Wonderful Pump

by L. Frank Baum

This tale, another by L. Frank Baum, reminds us to be careful what we wish for.

Not many years ago, there lived on a stony, barren New England farm a man and his wife. They were **sober**, honest people, working hard from early morning until dark to enable them to secure a **scanty** living from their poor land.

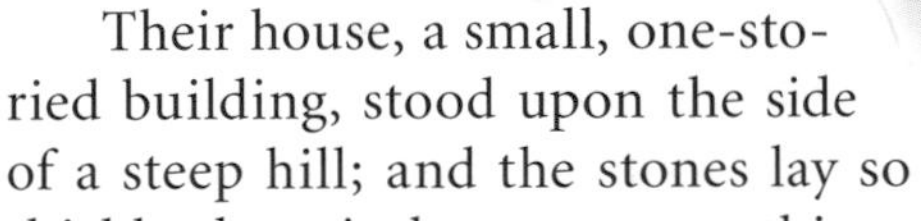

Their house, a small, one-storied building, stood upon the side of a steep hill; and the stones lay so thickly about it that **scarce** anything green could grow from the ground. At the foot of the hill, a quarter of a mile from the house by the winding path, was a small brook; and the woman was **obliged** to go there for water and to carry it up the hill to the house. This was a **tedious** task, and with the other hard work that fell to her share had made her gaunt and bent and lean.

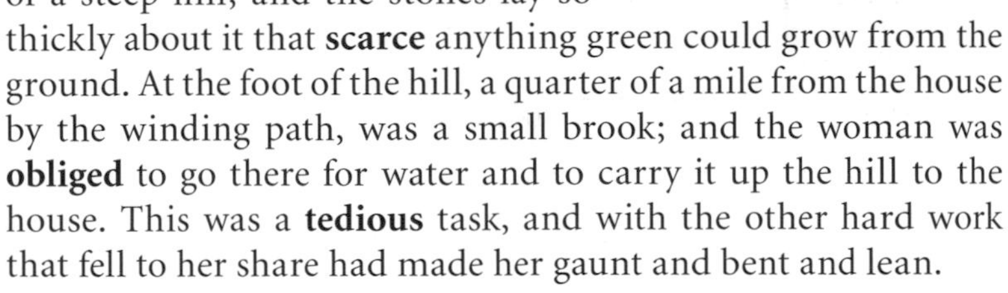

Yet she never complained, but meekly and faithfully performed her duties, doing the housework, carrying the water, and helping her husband hoe the scanty crop that grew upon the best part of their land.

One day, as she walked down the path to the brook, her big shoes scattering the pebbles right and left, she noticed a large beetle lying upon its back and struggling hard with its little legs to turn over, that its feet might again touch the ground. But this it could not accomplish; so the woman, who had a kind heart, reached down and gently turned the beetle with her finger. At once it scampered from the path, and she went on to the brook.

The next day, as she came for water, she was surprised to see the beetle again lying upon its back and struggling helplessly to turn. Once more the woman stopped and set him upon his feet; and then, as she stooped over the tiny creature, she heard a small voice say, "Oh, thank you! Thank you so much for saving me!"

Half frightened at hearing a beetle speak in her own language, the woman started back and exclaimed, "Lan sakes! Surely you can't talk like humans!"

Then, recovering from her alarm, she again bent over the beetle, who answered her, "Why shouldn't I talk, if I have anything to say?"

"'Cause you're a bug," replied the woman.

"That is true; and you saved my life—saved me from my enemies, the sparrows. And this is the second time you have come to my assistance, so I owe you a debt of gratitude. Bugs value their lives as much as human beings, and I am a more important creature than you, in your ignorance, may suppose. But, tell me, why do you come each day to the brook?"

"For water," she answered, staring stupidly down at the talking beetle.

"Isn't it hard work?" the creature inquired.

"Yes; but there's no water on the hill," said she.

"Then dig a well and put a pump in it," replied the beetle.

She shook her head.

"My man tried it once; but there was no water," she said sadly.

"Try it again," commanded the beetle; "and in return for your kindness to me I will make this promise: if you do not get water from the well you will get that which is more precious to you. I must go now. Do not forget. Dig a well."

And then, without pausing to say good-bye, it ran swiftly away and was lost among the stones.

The woman returned to the house much **perplexed** by what the beetle had said, and when her husband came in from his work she told him the whole story.

The poor man thought deeply for a time and then declared, "Wife, there may be truth in what the bug told you. There must be magic in the world yet, if a beetle can speak; and if there is such a thing as magic we may get water from the well. The pump I bought to use in the well that proved to be dry is now lying in the barn, and the only expense in following the talking bug's advice will be the labor of digging the hole. Labor I am used to; so I will dig the well."

Next day he set about it and dug so far down in the ground that he could hardly reach the top to climb out again; but not a drop of water was found.

"Perhaps you did not dig deep enough," his wife said, when he told her of his failure.

So the following day he made a long ladder, which he put into the hole; and then he dug, and dug, and dug, until the top of the ladder barely reached the top of the hole. But still there was no water.

When the woman next went to the brook with her pail, she saw the beetle sitting upon a stone beside her path. So she stopped and said, "My husband has dug the well; but there is no water."

"Did he put the pump in the well?" asked the beetle.

"No," she answered.

"Then do as I commanded; put in the pump, and if you do not get water I promise you something still more precious."

Saying which, the beetle swiftly slid from the stone and disappeared. The woman went back to the house and told her husband what the bug had said.

"Well," replied the simple fellow, "there can be no harm in trying."

So he got the pump from the barn and placed it in the well, and then he took hold of the handle and began to pump, while his wife stood by to watch what would happen.

No water came, but after a few moments a gold piece dropped from the spout of the pump, and then another, and another, until several handfuls of gold lay in a little heap upon the ground.

The man stopped pumping then and ran to help his wife gather the gold pieces into her apron; but their hands trembled so greatly through excitement and joy that they could scarcely pick up the sparkling coins.

At last she gathered them close to her bosom, and together they ran to the house, where they emptied the precious gold upon the table and counted the pieces.

All were stamped with the design of the United States mint and were worth five dollars each. Some were worn and somewhat discolored from use, while others seemed bright and new, as if they had not been much handled. When the value of the pieces was added together, they were found to be worth $300.

Suddenly the woman spoke.

"Husband, the beetle said truly when he declared we should get something more precious than water from the well. But run at once and take away the handle from the pump, lest anyone should pass this way and discover our secret."

So the man ran to the pump and removed the handle, which he carried to the house and hid underneath the bed.

They hardly slept a wink that night, lying awake to think of their good fortune and what they should do with their store of yellow gold. In all their former lives they had never possessed

more than a few dollars at a time, and now the cracked teapot was nearly full of gold coins.

The following day was Sunday, and they arose early and ran to see if their treasure was safe. There it lay, heaped snugly within the teapot, and they were so willing to feast their eyes upon it that it was long before the man could leave it to build the fire or the woman to cook the breakfast.

While they ate their simple meal, the woman said, "We will go to church today and return thanks for the riches that have come to us so suddenly. And I will give the pastor one of the gold pieces."

"It is well enough to go to church," replied her husband, "and also to return thanks. But in the night I decided how we will spend all our money; so there will be none left for the pastor."

"We can pump more," said the woman.

"Perhaps; and perhaps not," he answered, cautiously. "What we have we can depend upon, but whether or not there be more in the well I cannot say."

"Then go and find out," she returned, "for I am anxious to give something to the pastor, who is a poor man and deserving."

So the man got the pump handle from beneath the bed, and, going to the pump, fitted it in place. Then he set a large wooden bucket under the spout and began to pump. To their joy the gold pieces soon began flowing into the pail, and, seeing it about to run over the **brim**, the woman brought another pail.

But now the stream suddenly stopped, and the man said, cheerfully, "That is enough for today, good wife! We have added greatly to our treasure, and the parson shall have his gold piece. Indeed, I think I shall also put a coin into the contribution box."

Then, because the teapot would hold no more gold, the farmer emptied the pail into the wood-box, covering the money with dried leaves and twigs so that no one might suspect what lay underneath.

Afterward they dressed themselves in their best clothing and started for the church, each taking a bright gold piece from the teapot as a gift to the pastor.

Over the hill and down into the valley beyond they walked, feeling so happy and light-hearted that they did not mind the distance at all. At last they came to the little country church and entered just as the services began.

Being proud of their wealth and of the gifts they had brought for the pastor, they could scarcely wait for the moment when the deacon passed the contribution box. But at last the time came, and the farmer held his hand high over the box and dropped the gold piece so that all the congregation could see what he had given. The woman did likewise, feeling important and happy at being able to give the good parson so much.

The parson, watching from the pulpit, saw the gold drop into the box, and could hardly believe that his eyes did not deceive him. However, when the box was laid upon his desk, there were the two gold pieces; and he was so surprised that he nearly forgot his sermon.

When the people were leaving the church at the close of the services, the good man stopped the farmer and his wife and asked, "Where did you get so much gold?"

The woman gladly told him how she had rescued the beetle, and how, in return, they had been rewarded with the wonderful pump.

The pastor listened to it all gravely, and when the story was finished he said, "According to tradition strange things happened in this world ages ago, and now I find that strange things may also happen today. For by your tale you have found a beetle that can speak and also has power to bestow upon you great wealth."

Then he looked carefully at the gold pieces and continued, "Either this money is fairy gold or it is genuine metal, stamped at the mint of the United States government. If it is fairy gold it will disappear within twenty-four hours, and will therefore do no one any good. If it is real money, then your beetle must have robbed someone of the gold and placed it in your well. For all money belongs to someone, and if you have not earned it honestly, but have come by it in the mysterious way you mention, it was surely taken from the persons who owned it, without their consent. Where else could real money come from?"

The farmer and his wife were confused by this statement and looked guiltily at each other, for they were honest people and wished to wrong no one.

"Then you think the beetle stole the money?" asked the woman.

"By his magic powers he probably took it from its rightful owners. Even bugs that can speak have no **consciences** and cannot tell the difference between right and wrong. With a desire to reward you for your kindness, the beetle took from its lawful **possessors** the money you pumped from the well."

"Perhaps it really is fairy gold," suggested the man. "If so, we must go to the town and spend the money before it disappears."

"That would be wrong," answered the pastor; "for then the merchants would have neither money nor goods. To give them fairy gold would be to rob them."

"What, then, shall we do?" asked the poor woman, wringing her hands with grief and disappointment.

"Go home and wait until tomorrow. If the gold is then in your possession, it is real money and not fairy gold. But if it is real money you must try to restore it to its rightful owners. Take, also, these pieces that you have given me, for I cannot accept gold that is not honestly come by."

Sadly the poor people returned to their home, being greatly disturbed by what they had heard. Another sleepless night was passed, and on Monday morning they arose at daylight and ran to see if the gold was still visible.

"It is real money, after all!" cried the man; "for not a single piece has disappeared."

When the woman went to the brook that day, she looked for the beetle, and, sure enough, there he sat upon the flat stone.

"Are you happy now?" asked the beetle, as the woman paused before him.

"We are very unhappy," she answered; "for, although you have given us much gold, our good parson says it surely belongs to someone else, and was stolen by you to reward us."

"Your parson may be a good man," returned the beetle, with some indignation, "but he certainly is not overly wise. Nevertheless, if you do not want the gold I can take it from you as easily as I gave it."

"But we do want it!" cried the woman fearfully. "That is," she added, "if it is honestly come by."

"It is not stolen," replied the beetle **sulkily**, "and now belongs to no one but you. When you saved my life, I thought how I might reward you; and, knowing you to be poor, I decided gold would make you happier than anything else.

"You must know," he continued, "that although I appear so small and insignificant, I am really king of all the insects, and my people obey my slightest wish. Living, as they do, close to the ground, the insects often come across gold and other pieces of money that have been lost by men and have fallen into cracks or crevasses or become covered with earth or hidden by grass or weeds. Whenever my people find money in this way, they report the fact to me; but I have always let it lie because it could be of no possible use to an insect.

"However, when I decided to give you gold, I knew just where to obtain it without robbing any of your fellow creatures. Thousands of insects were at once sent by me in every direction to bring the pieces of lost gold to this hill. It cost my people several days of hard labor, as you may suppose; but by the time your husband had finished the well the gold began to arrive from all parts of the country, and during the night my subjects dumped it all into the well. So you may use it with a clear conscience, knowing that you wrong no one."

This explanation delighted the woman, and when she returned to the house and reported to her husband what the beetle had said, he also was overjoyed.

So they at once took a number of the gold pieces and went to the town to purchase provisions and clothing and many things of which they had long stood in need; but so proud were they of their newly acquired wealth that they took no pains to **conceal** it. They wanted everyone to know they had money, and so it was no wonder that when some of the wicked men in the village saw the gold they longed to possess it themselves.

"If they spend this money so freely," whispered one to another, "there must be a great store of gold at their home."

"That is true," was the answer. "Let us hasten there before they return and **ransack** the house."

So they left the village and hurried away to the farm on the hill, where they broke down the door and turned everything topsy turvy until they had discovered the gold in the wood-box and the teapot. It did not take them long to make this into bundles, which they slung upon their backs and carried off, and it was probably because they were in a great hurry that they did not stop to put the house in order again.

Presently the good woman and her husband came up the hill from the village with their arms full of bundles and followed by a crowd of small boys who had been hired to help carry the purchases. Then followed others, youngsters and country **louts**, attracted by the wealth and **prodigality** of the pair, who, from simple curiosity, trailed along behind like the tail of a comet and helped swell the **concourse** into a **triumphal** procession. Last of all came Guggins, the shopkeeper, carrying with much tenderness a new silk dress that was to be paid for when they reached the house, all the money they had taken to the village having already been lavishly spent.

The farmer, who had formerly been a modest man, was now so swelled with pride that he tipped the rim of his hat over his left ear and smoked a big cigar that was fast making him ill. His wife strutted along beside him like a peacock, enjoying to the full the **homage** and respect her wealth had won from those who formerly **deigned** not to notice her, and glancing from time to time at the admiring procession in the rear.

But, alas for their new-born pride! When they reached the farmhouse they found the door broken in, the furniture strewn in all directions, and their treasure stolen to the very last gold piece.

The crowd grinned and made slighting remarks of a personal nature, and Guggins, the shopkeeper, demanded in a loud voice the money for the silk dress he had brought...

Then the woman whispered to her husband to run and pump some more gold while she kept the crowd quiet, and he obeyed quickly. But after a few moments he returned with a white face to tell her the pump was dry, and not a gold piece could now be coaxed from the spout.

The procession marched back to the village, laughing and jeering at the farmer and his wife, who had pretended to be so rich; and some of the boys were naughty enough to throw stones at the house from the top of the hill. Mr. Guggins carried away his dress after severely scolding the woman for deceiving him, and when the couple at last found themselves alone their pride had turned to humiliation and their joy to bitter grief.

Just before sundown the woman dried her eyes and, having resumed her ordinary attire, went to the brook for water. When she came to the flat stone, she saw the King Beetle sitting upon it.

"The well is dry!" she cried out angrily.

"Yes," answered the beetle calmly, "you have pumped from it all the gold my people could find."

"But we are now ruined," said the woman, sitting down in the path, beginning to weep; "for robbers have stolen from us every penny we possessed."

"I'm sorry," returned the beetle, "but it is your own fault. Had you not made so great a show of your wealth, no one would have suspected you possessed a treasure, or thought to rob you. As it is, you have merely lost the gold that others have lost before you. It will probably be lost many times more before the world comes to an end."

"But what are we to do now?" she asked.

"What did you do before I gave you the money?"

"We worked from morning 'til night," said she.

"Then work still remains for you," remarked the beetle **composedly**; "no one will ever try to rob you of that, you may be sure!" And he slid from the stone and disappeared for the last time.

Vocabulary

sober: thoughtful

scanty: very small in size or amount

scarce: hardly

obliged: forced

tedious: boring

perplexed: confused

brim: the edge or rim of something

conscience: knowledge of right and wrong and a feeling one should do what is right

possessors: people who have or hold property; owners

sulkily: in an irritable way

conceal: to keep secret; to hide

ransack: to search through in order to rob

louts: rude people

prodigality: careless wastefulness

concourse: gathering

triumphal: joyful and proud

homage: honor

deigned: descended to a level that is beneath one's dignity

composedly: calmly

Comprehension Questions

1. How did the woman help the beetle?
2. What did the beetle do to show his gratitude?
3. What happened to the couple's fortune?
4. As far as the beetle is concerned, how could the couple have been sure to keep their fortune?

Extension Activity

Look up Proverbs 16:18 and write it. Then write a paragraph explaining how the verse applies to this story.

Unit 2
Davy Crockett

Excerpts from "Bear Hunting in Tennessee"

Davy Crockett

Born in 1786, Davy Crockett became an American hero for many reasons. He was a respected statesman, a great bear hunter and storyteller, and a heroic soldier in the Texas Revolution. However, because he was so well-loved, it is difficult to differentiate what he really did and said from what has been credited to him. Although Davy was eighteen before he learned to read and write, he wrote many excerpts about his life. The following is one of them—a brief account of one of his bear hunting adventures taken after he was defeated in a race for a position in the Tennessee State Legislature.

But the reader, I expect, would like to know a little about my employment during the two years while my **competitor** was in Congress. In this space I had some pretty tuff times, and will relate some few things that happened to me. So here goes, as the boy said when he run by himself. In the fall of 1825, I concluded I would build two large boats and load them with pipe **staves** for market. So I went down to the lake, which was about twenty-five miles from where I lived, and hired some men to assist me and went to work. Some built boats, and others got staves. I worked with my hands till the bears got fat. Then I turned to hunting, to lay in a supply of meat. I soon killed and **salted** down as many as

were necessary for my family, but about this time, one of my old neighbors who had settled down on the lake about twenty-five miles from me, came to my house and told me he wanted me to go down and kill some bears in his parts. He said they were extremely fat, and very plenty. I know'd that when they were fat, they were easily taken, for a fat bear can't run fast or long. But I asked a bear no favors, no way, for I now had eight large, fierce dogs. A bear stood no chance at all to get away from them. So I went home with him, and then I went on down towards the Mississippi River and **commenced** hunting.

We were out two weeks, and in that time killed fifteen bears. Having now supplied my friend with plenty of meat, I engaged occasionally again with my hands in our boat building and getting staves. But at length, I couldn't stand it any longer without another hunt. So I concluded to take my little son, cross over the lake, and take a hunt there. We got over; and that evening, we turned out and killed three bears in little or no time. The next morning, we drove up four **forks** and made a sort of **scaffold**. On this, we salted up our meat, so as to have it out of the reach of the wolves, for as soon as we would leave our camp, they would take possession. We had just eaten our breakfast when a company of hunters came to our camp that had fourteen dogs. These dogs were in such poor condition that when they would bark they would almost have to lean up against a tree and take a rest. I told them their dogs couldn't run in smell of a bear; and they had better stay at my camp and feed them on the bones I had cut out of my meat. I left them there and cut out, but I hadn't gone far when my dogs took a first-rate start after a very large fat old he-bear, which run right plump towards my camp. I pursued on, but my other hunters had heard my dogs coming and met them, and killed the bear before I got up with him. I gave him to them and cut out again for a creek called Big Clover, which wasn't very far off.

Just as I got to Big Clover, my dogs all broke and went ahead. In a little time, they raised a fuss, and all seemed to be going every way. I listened a while and found my dogs was in two groups, and that both was in a snorting fight. I sent my little son to one group, and I broke for the other. I got to mine first and found my dogs had a two-year-old bear down, so I just took out my big butcher knife, went up and slapped it into him, and killed him without shooting. There was five of the dogs in my company. In a short time, I heard my little son fire at his bear. When I went to him, he had killed it, too. He had two dogs in his team. Just at this moment we heard my other dog barking a short distance off, and all the rest immediately ran to him. We pushed on, too; and when we got there, we found he had still a larger bear than either of them we had killed, treed by himself. We killed that one also, which made three we had killed in less than half an hour. We turned in and butchered them, and then started to hunt for water and a good place to camp. But we had no sooner started than our dogs took a start after another one, and away they went like a **thunder gust**. We followed the way they had gone for some time, but at length we gave up the hope of finding them and turned back. As we were going back, I came to where a poor fellow was **grubbing**, and he looked like the very picture of hard times. I asked him what he was doing away there in the woods by himself. He said he was grubbing for a man who intended to settle there. The reason was that he had no meat for his family, and he was working for a little.

I was mighty sorry for the poor fellow, for it was not only hard, but it was a very slow way to get meat for a hungry family. I told him if he would go with me, I would give him more meat than he could get by grubbing in a month. I intended to supply him with meat, and also to get him to assist my little boy in packing in and salting up my bears. He had never seen a bear killed in his life. I told him I had six killed then, and my dogs were hard after another. He went off to his little cabin, which was a short distance in the brush; and his wife was very anxious he should go with me. So we started and went to where I had left my three bears and made a camp. We then gathered my meat and salted it, as I had done the other. Night now came on, but no word from my dogs yet. Afterwards, I found they had treed the bear about five miles off, near a man's house, and had barked at it the whole enduring night. Poor fellows! Many a time they looked for me, and wondered why I didn't come, for they knowed they could trust me, and I know they were as good as ever **fluttered**. In the morning, as soon as it was light enough to see, the man took his gun and went to them, shot the bear, and killed it. My dogs, however, wouldn't have anything to say to this stranger; so they left him and came back to me early in the morning.

We got our breakfast and cut out again. We killed four large and very fat bears that day. We hunted out the week; and in that time, we killed seventeen, all of them first-rate. When we closed our hunt, I gave the man over a thousand weight of fine fat bear-meat, which pleased him mightily, and made him feel as rich as a king. I saw him the next fall, and he told me he had plenty of meat to do him the whole year from his week's hunt. My son and me now went home. This was the week between Christmas and New Year that we made this hunt.

Vocabulary

competitor: someone who is in competition; in this case, referring to the man who beat him in his run for Tennessee representative

staves: narrow strips of iron plates placed edge to edge to form the sides of a boat

salted: preserved meat by rubbing salt on it

commenced: began

forks: tools used for digging

scaffold: a platform built as a support for workers

thunder gust: a sudden rush of wind and sound

grubbing: to clear by digging up roots and stumps

fluttered: to be anxious, nervous or worried

Comprehension Questions

1. A *dialect* is the way someone speaks (pronunciation, grammar, and vocabulary) based on where he lives. In "Bear Hunting in Tennessee," Davy Crockett writes in a southern dialect. Did the southern dialect add to the charm of the story? Or did the dialect make it more difficult to understand? Explain your answer.
2. How did Davy Crockett help the poor man that he met?

Be Sure You're Right, Then Go Ahead

Lawton B. Evans

This selection explains how Davy Crockett came to be involved in the Battle of the Alamo.

At one time, Texas was a part of Mexico; but the people of Texas did not like the rule of the Mexican government and rose in revolt to have their own independent state. This brought on a war between Texas and Mexico that lasted for several years. The Mexicans sent an army into Texas, and the Texans organized their own forces to resist the invasion. All this took place before Texas became a part of the United States.

At the time that Texas was fighting for independence, there was living in Tennessee a sturdy and heroic man by the name of David Crockett. He had lived in a cabin upon the frontier and had grown up as sturdy and as strong as the oaks in his own forests. He was very popular with the people who had elected him to several offices and even sent him to Congress. There he attracted a great deal of attention by his fearless and honest character, the simplicity of his manners, and his **unassuming** dress. Wherever he went he attracted attention. His motto was: "Be sure you're right, then go ahead."

He was a great admirer of Andrew Jackson and a friend of that statesman, but at one time he said, "I am willing to go with General Jackson in everything I believe right and honest, but beyond that I will not go for any man in creation."

Thus it was that David Crockett was known all over his state as a man that was afraid of nothing and that would not knowingly do wrong under any circumstances.

He opposed General Jackson in several matters and lost his popularity with the people of Tennessee. Crockett was defeated for public office and said, "Since my state no longer wishes my services, I have made up my mind to go to Texas. My life has been one of danger and hardship, and I should like to fight the Mexicans awhile."

He took his rifle, that he had named Betsy, and started on foot for Texas. He kissed his wife and children good-bye, telling them he would be back after a while. He was as tenderhearted as he was brave; and when he turned back to wave his hand to them, tears came into his eyes. He did not know then that he was seeing them for the last time.

He made his way slowly, sometimes on foot, sometimes on horseback, sometimes alone, and then again in the company of others traveling the same way. As he went along, he persuaded others to go with him and join the Texas army. On they went over the prairies bright with flowers and with the green grass of the springtime. Once they saw a **drove** of wild horses, and at night often heard the howling of wolves around their little camp.

One day as usual, the party stopped under some trees for dinner. They built a fire and cooked their midday meal. There was a low rumbling sound in the distance that was like the coming of a storm. Toward the west there appeared something like a dark cloud upon the horizon. The cloud approached rapidly and turned out to be a herd of buffalo that was coming toward the camp. The **bellowing** of the animals was like low thunder.

The men sprang up alarmed and were ready to mount their horses and flee for their lives. The horses themselves were frightened, and it was as much as the men could do to prevent them from stampeding.

On came the buffaloes with the speed of the wind. There were countless numbers of them. In those days the buffaloes on the plain were very numerous and traveled in great bands, and anything that was in their way was in immediate danger of being trampled to death. It seemed as if the travelers themselves were in such danger.

There was one great buffalo that led the herd. He was the leader or master. He came bellowing, with his head down. He was not more than a few hundred yards away from the startled travelers. Crockett saw that the only way to save the camp and his friends was to **divert** the leader from his **headlong** charge. Afterwards he said, "It was a beautiful sight. I had never had such a great chance in my life. I raised my rifle Betsy to my shoulder and blazed away at the buffalo as he came charging down upon us. I hit him in the shoulder. He stopped and raised his head. Then he pawed the ground and seemed undecided what to do next. Instead of charging us, he swerved to one side and went around the grove and was followed by the rest of the herd. It was a great sight and a narrow escape. Whether he fell later on, I could not tell."

The next day, they fell in with still another herd of buffalo; and Crockett was so excited by the prospect that he could not **forbear** to give chase. Mounting his horse, he left his companions behind and followed in the wake of the great moving mass. He did not look to see in what direction he was going but urged his horse on with whip and spur trying to keep up with the thundering herd. But the buffalo is a very swift runner, and the herd sped over the plain faster than Crockett could follow them. Soon they disappeared in the distance, and Crockett's horse was too tired to pursue them further. He looked around and discovered to his surprise and dismay that he was out of sight of his camp and had no idea in which direction to find it. He was lost upon the plain.

All afternoon he rode, hoping to find his way back, and at night camped under the stars. In the morning, he found that his horse had broken loose and strayed away. There he was alone on foot in the vast prairie. He was without water and without food.

He afterwards said he felt as he imagined a man would feel, adrift in a small boat in the middle of the ocean without any oars. He sat down to think what he should do. Then he saw some horsemen coming across the plains. He stood up and waved his coat to attract their attention. They turned out to be a band of Indians

who, when they came near, made friendly signs. Crockett was overjoyed to find himself in the hands of friends who took him in charge. Several days after that, the Indians supplied him with a horse and food and started him on his way again. Strange to say, he overtook his companions and, with them, continued on his way to Texas.

At length, they came to San Antonio where the famous fort called the **Alamo** stood in the heart of the town. There was a large Mexican force attacking the town, and the Texans were few in number. But David Crockett and his companions were not alarmed by the size of the enemy.

"Here I am," said he to the Texas leader. "I have Betsy with me; and every time she blazes, some Mexican is going to bite the dust."

He was welcomed to the company, you may be sure. After much fighting, the Texans took refuge in the Alamo. The siege was begun, and there was desperate fighting for several days. At last, the fortress was taken by overwhelming numbers, and one by one the brave Texans were slain.

David Crockett was among the last of those to lose their lives. Many Mexicans had fallen before his **unerring** marksmanship, and his rifle Betsy had done noble service in the cause of liberty. When the Mexicans made their way into the fort, he seized his rifle and laid about him with great strength and many went down before it. He sprang at the throat of the Mexican leader, hoping to choke him to death; but a dozen bullets were fired at him, and he fell dead along with his other companions. It was a heroic defense, long to be remembered in the history of Texas. And David Crockett will always be remembered by his countrymen on account of his honesty and bravery and his inspiring words: "Be sure you're right, then go ahead."

None of us can be sure he is right; but we can be sure of what we think is right, and then we should go ahead and do what we think we ought to do. The world never forgives one for doing what he knows is wrong, but is very patient with one who does what he thinks is right, though he may be making a mistake.

Vocabulary

unassuming: modest; shy

drove: a group of animals driven or moving in a body

bellowing: deep, loud roaring

divert: to distract; to turn the attention away

headlong: headfirst; with the head foremost

forbear: to hold back or keep from

Alamo: a Spanish mission, built in 1718

unerring: making no errors; unfailing

Comprehension Questions

1. How did Davy Crockett wind up lost on the plain? Who helped him? How?
2. How does "Be Sure You're Right, Then Go Ahead," explain the death of Davy Crockett?

Sally Ann Thunder Ann Whirlwind Crockett Bests Mike Fink

S.E. Schlosser

The following tall tale is about Davy Crockett's fictional wife, Sally Ann Thunder Ann Whirlwind Crockett. Read to find out what happens when she meets up with Mike Fink, an actual fisherman, who has a rough and tough reputation.

Half of the tall tale legendary couple, Davy Crockett done married the prettiest, the **sassiest**, the toughest gal in the West, don't ya know! Her name was Sally Ann Thunder Ann Whirlwind, and she was all that and then some! She was tougher than a grumpy she-bear and faster than a wildcat with his tail on fire and sweeter than honey, so that even hornets would let her use their nest for a **Sunday-go-to-Meeting hat**.

Naturally, Davy Crockett was proud of his wife and liked to boast about her skills. "Yes sir, she can wrestle an alligator until it gets down on its knees and begs for mercy," he told everyone. Well, Mike Fink, that tough old Mississippi roarer, **snag-lifter**, and **flatboat skuller**, took a dislike to Davy Crockett's boasting about his wife (maybe on account of his wife weren't half so tough), and he tried seven ways to Sunday to scare her good and proper. 'Course, Sally Ann Thunder Ann Whirlwind Crockett didn't pay any attention to his **antics**, and Davy Crockett about laughed 'til he busted to see Mike Fink trying to pull a fast one on her.

Finally, Mike Fink bet Davy Crockett a dozen wildcats that he could scare Miz Crockett until her teeth came loose and her toenails went out-of-joint. Davy Crockett figured this was an easy win, so he took the bet.

Well, Mike Fink took the skin of a mighty big alligator and wrapped it around himself. Then he crept into the bushes and waited until Sally Ann Thunder Ann Whirlwind Crockett came strolling by for her evening walk. Mike Fink leapt out of the brush and started a growling and a howling and roaring so loud he about scared himself out of his wits. But not Miz Crockett;

no, sir! She put her hands on her hips and **smirked** at that raging critter like it was a misbehavin' child.

That made Mike Fink pretty mad. He was determined to scare the wits outta Sally Ann Thunder Ann Whirlwind Crockett if it was the last thing he did. He stretched out the claws on that 'gater skin and started walking toward Miz Crockett, reaching to pull her into its deadly embrace. Now it was Sally Ann Thunder Ann Whirlwind Crockett's turn to get mad.

"Don't you be fresh!" she told that crazy critter. She gave him a glare so full of lightning that it lit up the sky from here to California, but Mike Fink kept a-coming 'cause he was determined to win the bet.

Sally Ann Thunder Ann Whirlwind Crockett took out a small toothpick that she carried with her to keep her smile all clean and pretty after she ate. She jest lit out with that toothpick and knocked the head right off that alligator skin. It whirled up and away about fifty feet into the air, and it took all the hair on top of Mike Fink's head right along with it. So now Mike Fink was left standing in front of Miz Crockett with a half-bald head and the remains of an alligator skin clutched around him.

Sally Ann Thunder Ann Whirlwind Crockett was not amused when she realized the famous Mississippi roarer was trying to scare the dickens out of her. She put away the toothpick, since she figured it gave her an unfair advantage, and proceeded to knock the stuffing out of Mike Fink until he fainted away in his alligator skin. Dusting off her hands, she glared down at his still form and said, "Good riddance!" and marched off to tell her husband the story. Davy Crockett laughed so hard he nearly split a **gusset**!

When folks asked Mike Fink how he got so busted up the next day, he told them he'd been chewed up and swallowed whole by an alligator. But he didn't fool Davy Crockett none with this story, so he had to give him a dozen wildcats to pay off his bet.

Mike Fink never messed with Miz Crockett again!

Vocabulary

sassiest: boldest; given to back talk

Sunday-go-to-Meeting hat: refers to a fine hat worn to church on Sundays

snag-lifter: referring to one who works with a snag, a riverboat similar to a barge

flatboat skuller: referring to one who works with a flatboat, a boat with a flat bottom and square ends used on rivers for carrying freight

antics: wildly playful or funny acts

smirked: smiled in an insincere manner

gusset: a triangular or diamond-shape piece of fabric sewn into the underarms of a garment to provide more freedom of movement

Comprehension Questions

1. What was Davy Crockett and Mike Fink's bet about in "Sally Ann Thunder Ann Whirlwind Crockett Beats Mike Fink"?
2. Who won the bet? Explain.
3. Tall tales include exaggerations, or details that could not happen in real life. Name an exaggeration in this tall tale.

Extension Activity

A cinquain is a pattern poem. Write a cinquain about Sally Ann Whirlwind using the following format.

Line 1: Name of character

Line 2: Two adjectives describing the character

Line 3: Three action verbs that relate to the character

Line 4: a phrase of four words that relates to the character

Line 5: One word that sums up the character

Here is a cinquain written about Paul Bunyan.

Example:

Paul Bunyan
Giant, strong
Chopping, sawing, hauling
Had a big crew
Lumberjack

Unit 3
The War of 1812

The War of 1812

Mara L. Pratt

Do you know the cause of the War of 1812? Read on to find out!

"Taxation without representation" was the cause of the American Revolution—a long phrase for little folks to remember, but easy enough after you understand what it means.

I shall have to ask you to remember a longer phrase, but I will try to explain it to you so that it will be as easy as that giving the cause of the Revolution.

The cause of this second war with England was "the **impressment** of American sailors and the capturing of our vessels."

Now let us see if we can understand what impressment of American sailors means.

Of course, England did not feel very kindly towards the American colonies after the Revolution. Not only had she met with a most humiliating defeat from those whom she had laughed at and called barnyard soldiers, **clod-hopper militia**, and many other such **contemptuous** names, but she had also lost a very valuable colony, one that would have been a source of great wealth to her as it grew in numbers and in power.

Ever since the Constitution had been formed, and the American nation had seemed so full of success, England had been doing everything possible to injure American **commerce**. England had for a long, long time called herself the "Mistress of the Sea," and had prided herself on having the finest navy in the world.

The United States, dreading to go to war again, had borne many an insult both from England and from France. But when the English began impressing American sailors—that was a little more than America could endure.

It had long been the custom in England to fill up their ships' crews by impressment, as they called it. This is the way they went about it. When they could not find enough men who were willing to become sailors, a party of rough men, called the "press-gang," would go upon land, look about for hearty, strong-looking young men, and, when they had found one who seemed likely to make a good sailor, would seize upon him, bind him, and carry him off to a ship.

Sometimes they did not seize upon these men, but would invite one to drink with them; and then when they had made him drunk, would carry him off to their vessel, throw him into the hold, and leave him there until he became sober. Many a poor lad had awakened from his **stupor** to find himself on shipboard, away from home and friends, bound on a voyage which was, perhaps, to last for years. If he refused to work, he was whipped until he cried for mercy. The "press-gang" was indeed the terror of all Europe. You see now what impressment of sailors means; just simply this: stealing them and forcing them to become sailors on English ships.

And now, when I tell you that thousands of Americans had been seized in just this way by these English ships, do you wonder that again America declared war against England?

It was just at the close of Jefferson's Administration that an event occurred that aroused the Americans to act at once.

As the *Chesapeake*, an American vessel, was crossing the ocean, it was ordered by the *Leopard*, an English vessel, to stop.

"I order you to stand and be searched," said the English officer.

"What do you expect to find?" asked Captain Barron.

"I search for English sailors," was the reply.

"We have no English sailors on board, and we shall not stop," answered the American captain.

"You are all Englishmen, and in the name of the English government, I demand that you be searched." Immediately the English ship fired upon the *Chesapeake*, killing and wounding several of the crew. Three sailors were taken from the vessel and forced to serve as slaves. Such outrages as this were enough to stir the anger of any nation; and if ever war was right, it was right in such a time as this.

But in spite of all this, the **Federalists** were opposed to war with England. They declared that if war with England was entered into, the United States would surely fall into the power of France, who was still at war with England.

It was just here that Henry Clay and John C. Calhoun, two of the greatest statesmen that America ever had, came into notice. Henry Clay was the leader of the Federalists, and was opposed to the war; John C. Calhoun was the leader of the Republicans, and was in favor of war.

Thus matters stood, when, in June 1812, Congress declared war with England.

Great was the joy in the hearts of these impressed sailors on the English ships. Many of them at once refused to pull another rope on board a ship belonging to a nation at war with their own country.

"Will you do your duty on this ship?" asked one captain of an American who was suffering under the lash for refusal to work the ship.

"Yes, sir," answered the man, with his back bleeding at every pore. "It is my duty to blow up this ship, an enemy to my country, and if I get a chance, I'll do it."

The captain looked round in astonishment. "I think this man must be an American," he said. "No English sailor would talk like that. He is probably crazy, and you may untie him and let him go."

Over 2,500 Americans who had been impressed and who thus refused to serve were sent to prison in England, where they were kept in the most **wretched** imprisonment until the war closed.

Many of the men were flogged—some of them till they dropped dead—but they showed the same brave spirit that they had shown years before in the Revolution. One would suppose that after being so completely defeated by the American colonies England would hardly have cared to go to war with the American states.

Vocabulary

impressment: forcibly taking recruits for millitary service

clod-hopper militia: an army made up of clumsy, unsophisticated people

contemptuous: disrespectful

commerce: business; trade

stupor: drunken state

Federalists: a major political party in the early years of the United States favoring a strong, centralized national government

wretched: horrible

Comprehension Questions

1. Explain what is meant by "the impressment of American sailors."
2. Explain why the Federalists did not want to declare war on England.
3. How did the impressed sailors show bravery?

Extension Activity

Write a paragraph about ONE of the following subjects concerning the War of 1812:

The impressment of American sailors during the War of 1812

The Embargo Act of 1813

The Battle of New Orleans

The burning of Washington, D.C.

The Treaty of Ghent

Use the following websites to research your topic:

- ⇨ http://www.warof1812.ca/1812events.htm
- ⇨ https://kidskonnect.com/history/war-1812/
- ⇨ http://www.socialstudiesforkids.com/subjects/warof1812.htm
- ⇨ http://americanhistory.pppst.com/warof1812.html

Old Ironsides

Lawton B. Evans

"Old Ironsides" was the nickname given to a great ship, the Constitution, *during the War of 1812. Read on to find out how the ship got this nickname.*

Part I

The good ship *Constitution* was built by order of Congress to fight the pirate ships of Algeria. She was built in Boston, and was designed to be a little bigger and a little better than any other fighting ship of her kind afloat.

The *Constitution* was made of the best material and with the greatest care. Workmen searched the lumberyards of the South for oak, cedar, and pine. Paul Revere, who made the famous midnight ride, furnished the copper. It took three years to build the **frigate**, and, when she was done, her **timbers** had seasoned until they were hard as iron.

The *Constitution* played her part in the war against the pirates of the Barbary Coast in Africa. For two years there was plenty of fighting, in which the frigate seemed to bear a charmed life. She never lost her mast, nor was she ever seriously injured in battle or in storm. She never lost a commanding officer, and only a few of her crew were killed.

It was during the War of 1812 that the *Constitution* won her chief glory. Her most remarkable feat was her escape from a British **squadron**. At daybreak, toward the middle of July 1812, off the New Jersey coast, the frigate found herself surrounded by a fleet of British ships that had crept up in the night. They were waiting for dawn to begin the attack. Captain Isaac Hull was in command of the *Constitution* and had no idea of surrendering his ship. He thought only of means to escape from his danger.

Not a breath of air ruffled the water, and the sails of all the ships were useless. One of the British frigates was being towed by all the boats of her squadron, so as to get her near enough to the *Constitution* to open fire. The boats then expected to bring other frigates into position, and thus begin a general battle. This would seal the doom of the *Constitution*. Without wind, there was no chance for her to get away. But Hull was not to be caught. He thought of his anchor and **windlass**.

"How much water have we under this ship?" he shouted. Upon being told he had twenty **fathoms**, he cried out, "Bring up the anchor and all the spare ropes and cable. Then all hands to the boats!"

The order was quickly obeyed. Putting the anchor into a boat, it was carried a mile ahead and dropped into the ocean. The ropes and cables attached to it were still fastened to the windlass. The men on the ship began to wind up the windlass, and gradually drew the boat along to the place where the anchor was dropped.

Then the anchor was moved ahead another mile, and the boat drawn up again. In this manner, slow progress was made through the water, but it was better than not making any headway at all.

The **pursuit** was kept up for two days. But slowly the *Constitution* gained distance from her pursuers, until, after a two days' chase, the enemy was four miles **astern**.

A **squall** gave Hull his chance to open sails and hide behind the rain and cloud banks. In a few hours, the weather cleared, and the British were almost out of sight. They soon abandoned the chase, and Hull took his frigate into Boston Harbor, amid the cheers of the people.

Part II

In less than two weeks, he was out again, searching the ocean for British craft, and ready to give battle to any vessel he might meet. The British had a fine frigate, named the *Guerriere*, commanded by Captain Dacres, who was a personal friend of Captain Hull. The *Guerriere* had challenged any vessel of the American fleet to battle and was cruising on the Atlantic, waiting for an answer. The *Constitution* went out to accept the challenge.

Years before this, Dacres and Hull had been talking about a possible battle between their frigates. "If we ever meet in combat, I **wager** a fine hat I will make you surrender," said Dacres to Hull.

"Agreed," was the laughing reply of Captain Hull. "I expect to win that hat someday."

In August, about 700 miles from Boston, the two vessels met. The *Constitution* and the *Guerriere* were the finest frigates in the world, their commanders equally brave, their men equally matched. It was a question of ship management and gun power.

The British frigate flung out a flag of **defiance** from each topmast. Her guns began to roar, but the balls fell short of the *Constitution.*

"Don't fire until I give the word. Let the two vessels draw near together before we open. Keep steady and ready, and never mind their guns," said Hull to his men.

The two ships drifted nearer and nearer. The enemy's **broadsides** tore through the rigging of the *Constitution.* One of the enemy's balls struck the side of the vessel and fell into the sea. A sailor, looking overboard, said, "See the balls falling away from her? She's an old ironside, sir, an old ironside."

From that time on, the *Constitution* was called "Old Ironsides."

The two vessels came fairly abreast, near enough for the men to see each other, and for good pistol shot.

"Ready, men, do your full duty and fire," shouted Hull.

Broadside after broadside was poured into the *Guerriere.* First her **mizzenmast** fell, then her foremast was cut down, then her rigging and flag; she was soon a helpless hulk in the water.

Dacres surrendered and came on board the *Constitution* to deliver his sword to his old friend. But Hull smilingly said, "No, Dacres, you can keep the sword, for you are too brave a man to be without one. I want that hat you and I wagered some years ago."

When "Old Ironsides" sailed into Boston on the last day of August, you may well believe the people shouted themselves hoarse, and waved flags, and hung out **bunting**, and gave grand dinners in honor of this great naval victory.

Vocabulary

frigate: a medium-sized warship

timbers: wood used for building a ship

squadron: a unit of ships

windlass: a machine on a ship used for pulling and lifting

fathom: about six feet

pursuit: chase

astern: behind

squall: a sudden violent wind, often with rain

wager: bet

defiance: challenge

broadsides: a firing of all guns on the same side of a ship

mizzenmast: the mast just behind the main mast of a ship

bunting: flags and other patriotic decorations

Comprehension Questions

1. In Part I, how did Captain Hull get away from the British squadron?
2. In Part II, what did Captain Dacres, the captain of the British ship the *Guerriere*, wager with Captain Hull?

3. Why did the nickname of the *Constitution* become "Old Ironsides"?
4. How did Captain Hull show mercy on Captain Dacres?

Extension Activities

1. Read the poem "Old Ironsides" by Oliver Wendell Holmes. You will find it on the following website:
   - ⇨ http://www.seacoastnh.com/ussconstitution/#list
2. Take the *Old Ironsides* Fun Quiz on page 3 of the *Student Exercises* booklet. Use the following websites for assistance:
   - ⇨ http://www.socialstudiesforkids.com/articles/ushistory/oldironsides.htm
   - ⇨ http://www.seahistory.org/assets/KIDS-120-22.pdf

The Star-Spangled Banner

Francis Scott Key

On September 13, 1814, Francis Scott Key was on an English ship. He was forced to be on an English ship because he was trying to get a doctor that was captured by the British out of their hands. Key had to stay on the ship throughout the night because of the orders of the captain of the ship. In doing so, he witnessed one of the most victorious battles in American history. At dawn, Key noticed that the huge American flag flying over Fort McHenry was still waving. He wrote a poem about what he witnessed that would later be set to music and become the National Anthem of The United States of America. While we might be well acquainted with the first verse, there are three more, just as moving.

Oh, say, can you see, by the dawn's early light,
What so proudly we hailed at the twilight's last gleaming?
Whose broad stripes and bright stars, thru the perilous fight,
O'er the **ramparts** we watched, were so gallantly streaming?
And the rockets' red glare, the bombs bursting in air,
Gave proof through the night that our flag was still there.
O say, does that star-spangled banner yet wave
O'er the land of the free and the home of the brave?

On the shore dimly seen through the mists of the deep,
Where the foe's **haughty** host in dread silence **reposes**,
What is that which the breeze, o'er the towering steep,
As it fitfully blows, half conceals, half discloses?
Now it catches the gleam of the morning's first beam,
In full glory reflected, now shines on the stream:
Tis the star-spangled banner: O, long may it wave
O'er the land of the free and the home of the brave!

And where is that band who so **vauntingly** swore
That the **havoc** of war and the battle's confusion
A home and a country should leave us no more?
Their blood has washed out their foul footsteps' pollution.
No refuge could save the **hireling** and slave
From the terror of flight or the gloom of the grave:

And the star-spangled banner in triumph doth wave
O'er the land of the free and the home of the brave.

O, thus be it ever when freemen shall stand,
Between their loved home and the war's **desolation**!
Blest with victory and peace, may the heav'n-rescued land
Praise the Power that hath made and preserved us a nation!
Then conquer we must, when our cause, it is just,
And this be our motto: "In God is our trust"
And the star-spangled banner in triumph shall wave
O'er the land of the free and the home of the brave!

Vocabulary

ramparts: a wall built for protection

haughty: overly proud

reposes: rests

vauntingly: proudly; boastfully

havoc: destruction

hireling: a worker

desolation: ruin

Extension Activity

Visit this interactive website to see Key's manuscript of the poem and more!

⇨ http://amhistory.si.edu/starspangledbanner/

Unit 4
Westward Ho!

The Old Miner's Story

Lawton B. Evans

Have you ever wondered what it would be like to discover gold? Beginning in 1848, many Americans took the long journey west in search of this precious metal. The following is a tale told by an old miner about his gold-seeking adventures as a boy.

At the time gold was discovered in California, San Francisco was a town of 700 **inhabitants**. The houses were small, built of wood, and clustered along the waterfront pretty much like any other frontier town. The streets were unpaved and often were ankle-deep in mud. In this **disorderly** fashion, there lived men who had come with their families across the plains or by ship, seeking any kind of fortune in the West. Some were looking for work on the ranch, some in the vineyards or orange groves, and others were mere adventurers, bound upon any kind of **exploit**.

When gold was discovered, the town went mad and everybody left for the diggings. Even the stores were shut up and the ships were abandoned and vessels lay in the harbor because the sailors had deserted them. The wild stories of wealth in the ground had set everybody crazy, and almost the whole population was off wandering through the hills, staking out **claims** and getting ready to dig for the precious metal.

It was more than a year before the great **throng** arrived to build San Francisco and start it on its way to the glorious town that it has since become. The first news of gold almost made it a **deserted** village, though later on thousands of people flocked into it, seeking temporary shelter when they also were on their way to the rich fields.

An old miner tells the story of how he came to California when he was a boy and was in San Francisco the day someone rode into town shouting aloud: "Gold has been discovered at Sutter's Fort. It is in the creek bottoms and in the dry beds and in the hills. Gold! Gold!" The rider might as well have cried that there was fire on the plains or that the Indians were on their way, for the **stampede** could not have been quicker or more complete.

Said the old miner, "I was but a boy, and I had come to California because I had nothing else to do. I had learned how to cook and do general chores for anybody that would provide me board and lodging. I joined a party of men who set out one morning for the gold fields. Not that I cared particularly for gold, because I would not know what to do with it if I had it. I was only a boy fourteen years old, but everybody was going so I went along.

"After several days hard traveling we came to a stream where a lot of men were digging the sand and pouring the gravel into buckets. This looked like hard work to me, and I did not see any gold. But I followed one of the men who carried the buckets of sand to something that looked very much like a cradle in which we used to rock the baby. He emptied the sand into this cradle and then poured water on it and rocked it back and forth and back and forth. Then he took the gravel out slowly, and to my surprise there were at the bottom of the cradle bright, shiny particles which he told me was gold.

"I could hardly believe my eyes when out of a single rocking of the cradle he could get enough particles to make half a teaspoonful of the precious metal.

"Some of the men who were digging in the bed of the stream did not have any cradle but only a large pan made of sheet iron. This pan was dipped into the bed of the stream and brought to the surface full of dirty gravel. Then the dirty gravel was washed, and the shiny particles of gold were carefully gathered.

"This was known as placer mining and was very wasteful, but it was the best the miners could do at first.

"I stood there watching the men, and I heard one of the men say, 'I guess you have got about twenty-five dollars' worth of gold this trip.' Another one said, 'I panned out more than one hundred dollars yesterday.' And still another spoke of several hundred dollars that he had made in one day. All this made my eyes open.

"Finally, one of the men said to me, 'Sonny, why do you stand there **idle**? Why don't you get a pan and go to washing? Why don't you get out your knife and go up on the side of the hill and dig in the ground and see if you can't find a claim of your own? They say these hills are full of gold.'

"I had no cradle and I had no pan, but I did have a big hunting knife in my pocket that I always carried with me, and just for amusement's sake I said to him, 'I will walk up this hill a few hundred yards and open a mine.'

"They all laughed, but nevertheless, I started up the hillside. As I went, it entered into my boyish mind that I may as well join in the mad rush for wealth. Suppose I should find a mine! Suppose I should open a pocket in the ground and find gold! At that moment the gold fever struck into my blood, and I caught it as all the others had done. I rushed up the hill in the same mad race as I had seen others do. I also had gone wild with the lust for gold that had made all the others leave home and comfort for what they might find in the hills.

"I crossed the hill and ran into a little valley and began to dig wildly with my pocket knife. There was nothing there. I ran on a few hundred yards and began to dig again. Nothing there. My spirits began to sink, and I wondered if the gold was anywhere except in the streams.

"I climbed up a small hill and came to an open place where the dirt was loose. There was a **boulder** across my path which I determined to push to one side just as many a time I had looked for worms under a rock before going fishing. I pushed the boulder loose from its bed and set it rolling down the hill. Then I looked on the ground, and my heart stood still. Underneath there were shining particles of gold. I had discovered a mine! I turned pale with excitement and could hardly keep from screaming aloud at the top of my voice, but I knew that I had to stake my claim in

order to own this land. So I cut some long sticks and drove them in the ground several hundred feet apart, making a square, and in my childish way I scrawled my name upon these stakes with my knife.

"I gathered up the particles that I had found in the bed of the boulder and **hastened** back to my companions and showed them what I had found. They opened their eyes in **astonishment**. 'Sonny, you have certainly found something worthwhile. These are nuggets. You have got five hundred dollars in your hands right now.' I remember those words very well.

"They went back with me, and in a kindhearted way agreed to my claim.

"Do you know that accidentally I had discovered one of the finest mines in California? And after taking out of it a **moderate** fortune, I was foolish enough to sell it to some **prospectors** who made more than a million dollars out of it?"

But the old miner seemed to be satisfied because he had enough for all his wants. "You see," said he with a wise philosophy, "no one man can make it all. I made my share out of that mine, and I passed it on to others to make their share. I guess that's about right."

Vocabulary

inhabitants: people who live permanently in a place

disorderly: not behaving well

exploit: a brave or daring act

claims: areas of land marked out by people who explore a region in search of gold

throng: a large number of people gathered in one area

deserted: abandoned; empty

stampede: a sudden movement of a crowd of people

idle: lazy; not willing to work

boulder: a large rock

hastened: hurried

astonishment: great surprise

moderate: average in size or amount

prospectors: people who explore a region in search of gold

Comprehension Questions

1. What happened when someone rode through San Francisco alerting people that gold was found at Sutter's Fort?
2. What did the miner discover? How did he discover it?
3. How did the miner stake his claim?
4. Was the miner satisfied with his discovery? Explain.

Extension Activity

Read information from the following website to learn more about the Gold Rush:

⇨ http://pbskids.org/wayback/goldrush/

What Ben Did to a Bear

Lawton B. Evans

Some folks who headed west got more adventure than they bargained for....

Ben Mosley had moved his family to California and had staked out a claim up in the hills. This was in the days when everybody was crazy over the discovery of gold and was expecting to dig a fortune out of the ground. Ben had done very well. He and his partner had found enough of the precious metal on the land he claimed to make him well satisfied with his **venture**.

He had come across the plains in a wagon along with about twenty other families, bringing his wife and two boys, riding his horse and driving his three cows. It had taken six months, but they had enjoyed the trip, had no accidents, and were strong and healthy.

He had a cheerful and happy wife who loved the new country and who loved Ben wherever he was, and who was always ready to do her part. They had a cabin up in the hills, not far from the diggings, where some vegetables and flowers grew, and where the boys played. Wood was abundant, the birds sang in the trees, and the air was full of sunshine, as were the hearts of the adventurers into the land of gold and glory.

The woods were full of game, and Ben was a deadly shot with his big, heavy rifle or his shotgun. Never was the cabin without its supply of squirrels or rabbits or birds, and larger game was brought in when needed for the winter days. There were deer in the valleys and on the hillsides, and bears in the mountains—grizzly bears at that.

Now the grizzly bear is one of the terrors of the mountains. He is an enormous fellow, with forearms strong enough to crush an ox if he could get around him. His big teeth can crack any bone or bite through any flesh. If he should once get a man in his great arms, he could squeeze him to death and bite his head off. He could kill one with a single blow of his mighty paws. He is the biggest and fiercest of the bears that live in the western hills.

Of course, Ben knew there were grizzly bears in the mountains, but he had never seen one; and he knew they never attacked a cabin. They were **timid** beasts, even if they were powerful. Therefore, he was not much alarmed.

However, he told Jane, his wife, "Be careful not to go too far from the cabin, and watch the boys, for some bear might think they are pigs and **devour** them."

Jane promised, saying, "Ben, you be careful, too. I don't want some bear to bring you home inside of him. I would not know what to do."

Ben laughed, took his big rifle, and went off into the woods to shoot a deer, for the meat supply was getting low. He took some food in his pocket and some chewing tobacco, for Ben loved to chew, as did most of the miners at that time.

He went through the woods farther and farther from the cabin, up the mountain side, along the trail, keeping an eye out for game. He watched the ground closely for deer tracks and was soon rewarded for his pains. The wind was blowing his way so that his scent was carried from any game in front of him. Cautiously, he made a turn around a shoulder in the mountain and caught sight of several deer feeding with their heads down.

Raising his rifle, he fired, and the buck fell while the doe ran away, swift as the wind. It was but a moment of time before Ben had reached the deer, put an end to him with his keen knife, and began to cut him up so that he could take some of the meat home and hang the rest in the trees. Well he knew that the coyotes and wolves would soon be around if he left any of it on the ground.

He had laid his rifle aside and was intent upon his work when he heard a low growl behind him. Turning, he saw to his amazement the great form of a grizzly bear standing over his rifle and showing his teeth in a most **menacing** way.

The bear seemed as astonished as Ben, and showed it by standing up on his hind legs and snarling as bears will when they come upon anything in their way. He was not hunting for Ben; but now that he had come across him, he did not seem in any humor to go back. In fact, the big beast showed every sign of getting ready to advance upon his sworn foe and of making one less man in the wilderness he thought was his own.

Ben's knife dropped from his hand. His gun was beyond reach; the bear had that covered. There was a low tree nearby, toward which Ben ran as fast as he could and barely was in its branches before the beast came lumbering and growling behind him. The tree was about ten feet high, but was the stump of a strong one that the wind had broken. Ben was safe, but a prisoner.

It was no comfort to him to see the bear go to the body of the deer and tear it to pieces with his teeth and scatter the bits around. It was no pleasure to see how the bear kept his eye on the prisoner up in the tree, just out of reach of him. It was with **dismay** that he saw the bear take the gun in his mouth and crack the **stock** in his teeth as though it were a twig. Ben was in a bad fix and he knew it. All he had was the food in his pocket and his tobacco, and that was no defense against a grizzly.

The bear showed no signs of going away. In fact, he sat down to a kind of **siege**, for there was plenty of time, since the day was young and there was no hurry.

"What if this beast keeps me here all day and all night? What will Jane think? And what will she do?" His thoughts were not pleasant.

"She will be worried, thinking I have been hurt or lost. Suppose she should start out to look for me and come this way."

Ben was more worried about Jane and the boys than he was about himself.

He took out the bread and meat from his pocket and began to eat it. He may as well be comfortable. The bear smelled the food and came nosing around the tree. Ben watched him closely. My, he was a big fellow; and his paws went click, click, as they struck the loose stones.

An hour, two hours passed, and the bear held on. He lay down at the foot of the tree, then stood up at its base. He could not reach Ben, but he could keep him there. The day wore on, and Ben grew sore and tired, and more and more worried.

He took out his tobacco, bit off a big piece, and began to chew it. Then an idea came to his mind. He would see how it worked on the bear. Something had to be done to get rid of the grizzly before night anyhow. He climbed down, just about a foot above the reach of the bear, as if he were going to descend.

This suited the grizzly exactly, and he rushed forward to meet him. Standing up his full length against the trunk, he opened his mouth wide and his eyes shone **balefully** at his prey. Now was Ben's chance. His mouth was full of tobacco. He lowered his head and spat right into both eyes of the bear, and then threw the rest of the tobacco down his throat.

It was the most astonished bear you ever saw. His eyes were closed with the pain of the juice of the tobacco, and what he had swallowed made him deathly sick. He rolled over on the ground, rubbing his eyes with his paws, and then with a howl and a growl stumbled off.

Ben did not lose any time. Down he came, gathered what was left of his gun, and made home as fast as he could. But he always laughed till he cried when he told about the time he tried to teach a grizzly to chew tobacco.

Vocabulary

venture: an undertaking involving chance, risk, or danger

timid: feeling or showing a lack of courage or self-confidence; shy

devour: to eat up greedily or hungrily

menacing: threatening

dismay: a loss of courage or a feeling of concern

stock: a part of a rifle or other firearm, to which the barrel is attached

siege: the placing of an army around a fortified place or city to force it to surrender

balefully: in a threatening way

Comprehension Questions

1. What was Ben's biggest worry when he was up in the tree?
2. When Ben was in the tree, what were the only items he had with him?
3. How did Ben use one of the items to defend himself?
4. How did the bear react at the end of the story?

Extension Activity

Choose one of the following writing projects:

Write a different ending to the story. Begin with Ben being up in the tree.

This story is written in third person, meaning there is a narrator telling the story. Rewrite the ending as if Ben is speaking, telling the story. Begin with Ben being up in the tree.

The Redwood Tells Its Story

Lawton B. Evans

Many of those who traveled west were in awe of the beautiful redwoods of California. What would the redwoods say if they could speak? Read on to find out!

We were in the redwood district of California and standing by the side of a great tree that loomed above us nearly 400 feet high. Its trunk was twenty feet thick and sixty feet around. As we looked up at the great monster and its tremendous **proportions**, we were lost in admiration of its magnificence and its solemn **splendor**. It stood silent and majestic. One of our party exclaimed, "I wonder how old is this redwood tree?"

A gentle wind blew down from the mountains and unsealed the lips of the giant redwood and then, strangely enough, it began to tell its tale. This is what the redwood said:

"You want to know how old I am? Well, I will tell you that I am not only the oldest living thing on the American continent, but I am the oldest living thing in the world. When Britain was still under **Saxon** rule, and before **Charlemagne** had **ascended** the German throne, I had begun my growth. That was 1,200 years ago, and I was a little sapling—not more than a few feet high, but I had begun to grow. For twelve centuries I have been adding year by year to my height and to my size, and I do not know that I have stopped growing yet.

"And I am not the oldest of the redwoods, either. I have heard others boast that they were 2,000 years old, and some say that they are as old as the pyramids of Egypt, way back yonder 3,000 years ago. When Columbus discovered America, I was 200 feet high, but he had no idea that I was way over here on this side of the continent. Around me were many companions that were growing as I was. Some of them were my size, but I was big and husky, with plenty of room around me, and I was outgrowing them all."

"And how did you get your name of Sequoia?" we asked.

"I am named Sequoia in honor of a Cherokee Indian that once lived in Georgia and who made the Cherokee alphabet so that the Cherokee Indians could read. In honor of this Indian they named me Sequoia. I am sometimes called *Sempervirens*, which means "living forever," and from the way I feel now, when I am 1,200 years old, I believe I shall still live another 1,200 years."

"And how do you compare with other things that man has built upon this continent?" we asked.

To this the redwood replied, "I am 100 feet taller than the Statue of Liberty, and there is no tree on this continent that is taller than I."

"And how do you measure your age?" we asked.

"It is this way: Every year I grow I make a small ring around the outside of my trunk. This is the only way that anyone can tell how old I am. Of course, you could not tell unless you were to cut me down and count the rings, which I hope you will never do. However, if you did you would find that there are about 1,200 of these rings. Each one is very small, but each represents a year's growth."

"Do men ever cut down the redwoods?" we asked, **sympathetically**.

"Ah, yes," replied the tree. "They do cut us down, and I am sorry that they are doing it. Of course, our wood is valuable. I think it is a pity that we should be cut down at all because it takes us so long to grow. Within a day, a few men can destroy a life that has lasted all these centuries. I remember how, when one of my companions was cut down and the trunk was sawed off for a museum, fifty-two men formed a circle and stood around the edge of the stump. Think of that! Fifty-two men standing on the stump of one tree and then not filling up the center."

We listened to what the redwood had to say and wondered at its size and admired its majesty. Then the redwood continued:

"I am glad the government is protecting a few of us in its national forests, and thank heaven I am one of them. I should hate to be cut down now when I expect to keep on living and growing until I may reach a height of 500 feet and live to be 2,000 years old. From my topmost branches I overlook all the forests and see the young trees growing around me, and I wish them well. I am the guardian of these mountains; I have looked over this landscape all these centuries, and I would miss my companions, and I know they would miss me if ever I am gone. I have withstood the strains of winter, the heat of summer, the rains and the drought, because my roots spread 100 feet just beneath the ground to the everlasting waters. Only man can destroy me. If I am left alone, I shall live for many more centuries."

We took off our hats to the great redwood. We felt small and **insignificant** in the presence of its **immense** size and height, and in the splendor of its age. We waved our hands to it in leaving and expressed our hope that in centuries to come, others might hear its story of the wonders of the things that it has seen.

Vocabulary

proportions: size

splendor: glory; a show of magnificence

Saxon: referring to the Anglo-Saxons, a race of Germanic people who ruled Britain until AD 1066

Charlemagne: king of the Francs from AD 768 and Emperor of the Romans from AD 800 until his death in AD 814

ascended: climbed

sympathetically: sensitively

insignificant: unimportant

immense: huge

Comprehension Questions

1. How did the Sequoia get its name?
2. The redwood says it is 100 feet taller than the Statue of Liberty (from her heel to the top of her head). How tall is that? Use an encyclopedia or the Internet to find out.
3. What does each ring on a tree represent?
4. List two other facts you have learned about giant redwoods from this selection.

Extension Activities

Complete the activities on pages 4-10 of the Student Exercises *workbook. The first activity is a biblical play about trees called* "Shhh!" Said the Trees, *which can be performed in a group setting. The second activity involves writing a research report about the redwoods.*

Unit 5
The Civil War

Clara Barton

By Gertrude van Duyn Southwerth

This short biographical excerpt will introduce you to an amazingly generous woman who began her most important work during the Civil War, also called The War Between the States.

Fort Sumter had been fired upon; and in response to Lincoln's call for troops, Massachusetts had sent a **regiment** to Washington. As the soldiers were passing through Baltimore, they were attacked by a mob. Some were killed, and forty were wounded.

Among the anxious crowd waiting about the Washington station for the arrival of the wounded men was Miss Clara Barton. Her heart was full of sympathy when she saw the suffering soldiers. She followed to where they were carried and gave up her time to nursing them. Hard as the work was, she liked it. And seeing how much she could do to help and comfort the sick soldiers, she nobly offered her services for as long as they might be needed.

The women of the North responded to Lincoln's call as promptly as the men. While the troops were gathering to defend the Union, the Northern women were rolling bandages, making **delicacies**, and collecting comforts to be sent to the front—a work that they kept up throughout the war.

That all these supplies might be handled wisely, the United States appointed the **Sanitary Commission**. With the money and necessities sent from the different Northern states and, above all, with the help of such women as Mary Livermore, Dorothy Dix, and Clara Barton, this Sanitary Commission did a wonderful work. Many a soldier, wounded in the battles of the West, was carried north on the Mississippi ambulance boat. Still others—and these in thousands—were cared for by nurses on the battlefield or in the camp hospital.

When the war was over, and Miss Barton was no longer needed to attend the country's injured soldiers, she went **abroad**. She was worn out and needed rest. In the course of her travels, she learned that the chief nations of Europe had organized the Red Cross Society and had pledged themselves to uphold it. The object of this society was to care for all sick or wounded soldiers needing help, whether friend or foe. It had adopted a flag—a red cross on a white background—the reverse of the flag of Switzerland, where the society had been organized; and it was agreed that even on the battlefield this flag should be respected by both sides alike.

What possibilities lay before such a society! Miss Barton, after her Civil War experience, easily saw what it could do; so she became a member of the Red Cross and served under its flag on European battlefields.

When at last she returned to America, it was with the determination to **induce** her country to sign the international agreement regarding the Red Cross Society. At this time the United States was at peace, and it was hard to interest people in a society to care for injured soldiers. But after five years of constant effort on Miss Barton's part, the Association of the American Red Cross was formed, with Clara Barton as its president. Not only did the American Red Cross Society pledge itself to the care of wounded soldiers in the time of war, it also agreed to render relief to the victims of any great national **calamity**.

Great calamities have, in one year and another, befallen the American nation since; and time and again the Red Cross Society

has worked to relieve the results of flood, fire, or pestilence. In May 1889, the breaking of a dam in western Pennsylvania was followed by a flood that nearly swept Johnstown out of existence. Houses were carried away, thousands of people were killed, and those who survived were homeless and without food. To this scene of desolation Miss Barton and her fellow Red Cross members went. And for five months they stayed, sometimes in tents, sometimes without shelter, distributing the money, food, and other supplies sent to the **afflicted** city.

Nor was this all. Six "Red Cross Hotels" were put up as quickly as possible, and here the homeless people were sheltered and fed. Three thousand houses were built by a general committee, and the Red Cross Society supplied each and every one of them with furniture and made them ready for use. When she went home, Miss Barton left behind her the beginnings of a new and grateful Johnstown.

Nine years later came the war with Spain. Spain owned several of the West Indian islands, Cuba among them; and the cruel treatment of the Spanish government had driven Cuba to revolt. For a while America watched the unequal struggle, and then the United States ordered Spain to give the Cubans their freedom. She refused, and American soldiers and sailors were sent to win for the Cubans what they could not win for themselves.

Even before America took a hand in Cuba's war, Clara Barton had visited the island and tried to relieve the terrible misery and starvation caused by Spanish **brutality**. Then, during the war, while the Red Cross flag waved over the army hospitals, the **plucky** nurses fed and nursed the wounded soldiers, helped the surgeons at their work, and comforted the dying.

Thirty-seven years lay between the opening of the War Between the States and the Spanish-American War. These thirty-seven years had changed Miss Barton from a young woman to a woman of nearly seventy. Yet she served as energetically, loyally, and unselfishly in Cuba as she had served the boys in blue and gray so many years before.

Through her efforts the Red Cross Society is now firmly planted in America, its members always ready to share the hardships and lessen the sufferings of the victims of future disasters. In years to come, as in years gone by, Americans will richly bless the name of Clara Barton.

Vocabulary

regiment: a military unit consisting of many troops

delicacies: something pleasing to eat; a treat

Sanitary Commission: a group founded in 1861 whose mission was to keep army camps clean and filled with supplies

abroad: to another country

induce: persuade

calamity: any event that causes great harm

afflicted: caused suffering

brutality: cruelty

plucky: brave; courageous

Comprehension Questions

1. How did many women help during the Civil War?
2. What was the mission of the Red Cross Society?
3. What did Clara Barton do when she returned to America after traveling abroad?
4. What role did Clara Barton play in the American Red Cross Society?
5. What second mission did the American Red Cross Society pledge itself to when it formed?
6. Summarize how the American Red Cross Society helped Johnstown, Pennsylvania, in May of 1889.
7. Summarize how the American Red Cross Society helped Cuba in 1898.

Extension Activity

Research and write a short paragraph about one of the following people mentioned in the story:

Mary Livermore

Dorothy Dix

For Further Reading

Clara Barton: Civil War Nurse by Nancy Whitelaw (128 pages)

Clara Barton: Founder of the American Red Cross by Augusta Stevenson. New York: Aladdin Paperbacks (192 pages)

Abraham Lincoln

Lawton B. Evans

This selection is a short biography of the sixteenth President of the United States.

Lincoln was born in a cabin, in a dreary region of the state of Kentucky. It was a one-room house, about fourteen feet square, built of logs. In this one room the family cooked, ate, and slept. Very few children have started life in so poor and **barren** a home as did Abraham Lincoln.

When he was seven years old, his parents moved to Indiana, into a wild and wooded region, and there built a **rude** place to live in. It was still a cabin, with the roughest of furniture. A log, smoothed on one side, was used as a table. The bedsteads were made of poles fastened to the walls. The chairs were blocks of wood. All the cooking was done in the fireplace.

Here Lincoln spent his childhood in toil and hardship. The family was poor, and every member had to do hard work on the farm. After laboring all day, the young boy would often lie down before the fireplace and read by the light of the burning fire. Then, when too tired to read any more, he would climb a ladder, made of pegs driven into the wall, and go to sleep in the loft on a **pallet** of straw, covered with skins.

He had but little chance to get an education. He did not go to school more than a year, all told, and had very poor teachers. But he learned to read such books as *Aesop's Fables*, *The Pilgrim's Progress*, and the Bible.

He borrowed the *Life of Washington* from a neighbor and sat up far into the night reading it. He kept it in a **crevice** in the wall, near his bed, for safety. One night it rained, and he found the book soaked through and through. The owner made him work three days to pay for it, and then let him have it. It was the first book the boy owned.

He was accustomed to hearing every preacher and **stump orator** that came into his neighborhood. Once he walked fourteen miles to hear a trial in court. When one of the lawyers finished his speech, Lincoln walked across the room in his bare feet, with his trousers rolled up, and said quite audibly, "I want to shake your hand. That is the best speech I ever heard." Years after, when Lincoln was President, the lawyer, grown old and feeble, came to the White House and reminded him of the incident.

When Lincoln was about twenty-one years of age, his father and two of his neighbors moved to Illinois. Through mud and water, and over rough roads, Lincoln walked all the way, driving an ox-team. They settled about ten miles from Decatur and started life afresh.

Lincoln aided in clearing the land, and he fenced it with rails. He helped build the cabins and plant the spring crops. Though he was of age, and could have done as he pleased, he stayed with the family until they had started in their new surroundings.

He needed some clothes, for he still wore the buckskins of the frontier. He bargained with a neighbor to make him a pair of trousers out of brown jeans, dyed with white walnut bark, agreeing to split rails in payment. He had to split 1,400 rails before the trousers were paid for.

Lincoln was now a grown man, six feet and four inches tall, thin, but muscular, and in perfect health. He was much beloved by the community in which he lived and was popular with his companions. He could out-run, out-jump, and out wrestle anybody in the neighborhood. And, as a rail-splitter, nobody could approach him in the number he could split a day, for he had **precision** and power with a sharp ax. Every blow fell in the right place, and with great force. To see him cut down a large tree, and split it into rails, was to witness an exhibition of rare skill.

He was also a good storyteller. All his life he had an **inexhaustible** supply of funny stories to fit any occasion. He gained a reputation for honesty and square dealing in all his business transactions. That is why he was called "Honest Abe." One day, a woman came into the store where Lincoln was engaged as clerk. After she had gone, he noticed that she had given him six cents too much. That night, after his job was finished, he walked five miles to the woman's house to return the money to her.

With hard study and hard work, Lincoln began to be a leader in the town of New Salem, where he was employed. He studied law, was admitted to the **bar**, and was elected to the Legislature. He was sent to Congress and was a candidate for the United States Senate.

As a lawyer, he was very shrewd and successful. Upon one occasion he defended the son of a poor woman, who was accused of murdering a man at night. Lincoln was satisfied in his own mind that the boy was innocent. The trial began, and the witnesses were called.

The chief witness said, "I saw him strike the man and kill him."

Lincoln inquired, "What time was it when you saw him?"

"It was about eleven o'clock," the witness replied.

"How could you see so well at night?" asked the lawyer.

The man replied, "The moon was shining, and I could easily see by its light."

Lincoln sent for an almanac and showed the jury that there was no moon shining on that night, whereupon the witness retired in confusion, and the man was **acquitted** of the crime.

In after years, Lincoln was President of the United States, during the trying period of the Civil War. His was a deep responsibility, and he felt the burden of saving the Union very keenly.

He was a man of strong convictions and of great firmness. He was cast by nature in a heroic mold, yet he was always sympathetic and tender in his dealings with men. His **disposition** was **melancholy**, in spite of his humor, and he **brooded** deeply over the welfare of the country. His great hope was to save the Union at any cost, and it grieved him profoundly to see the Southern states secede.

Vocabulary

barren: bare; not much furniture

rude: roughly made

pallet: mattress

crevice: a narrow opening caused by a split or crack

stump orator: one who likes to discuss politics

precision: exactness; accuracy

inexhaustible: impossible to use up

bar: official group of lawyers

acquitted: freed or cleared from a charge or accusation

disposition: one's usual mood

melancholy: sad or gloomy

brooded: worried

Extension Activity

Fill out the Understanding Character Traits chart on page 11 of the Student Exercises *booklet.*

Eddy the Drummer Boy

Mara L. Pratt

Can you imagine being part of the Union Army during the Civil War? In those days, the army enlisted boys as young as eight years old to play drums and fifes, or flutes. The music signaled troops to fire, retreat, advance, and so forth. The following is the story of Eddy, a Union drummer boy.

One of the saddest stories of the war is the story of little Eddy, the drummer boy.

His father, a Union man of East Tennessee, had been killed, and his mother had gone to St. Louis with Eddy, then about twelve years old, in hope of finding a sister who lived there. Failing in this, and running out of money, she applied to the captain of one of the companies in the Iowa First Infantry to get Eddy a position as drummer boy. The regiment had only six weeks longer to serve, and she hoped that during that time she might get work for herself and find her sister. The captain was about to say that he could not take so small a boy, when Eddy spoke out, "Don't be afraid, Captain, I can drum."

Upon this, the captain replied, with a smile, "Well, well, Sergeant, bring the drum, and order the fifer to come forward."

The fifer, a **lank**, round-shouldered fellow, more than six feet high, came forward; and bending down with his hands on his knees, asked, "My little man, can you drum?"

"Yes, sir," said Eddie, "I drummed for Captain Hill in Tennessee."

The fifer straightened himself up and played one of the most difficult tunes to follow with the drum; but Eddy kept pace with him through all the hardest parts and showed that he was a master of the drum.

"Madam, I will take your boy," said the captain. "What is his name?"

"Edward Lee," she replied, wiping a tear from her eye. "Oh! Captain, if he is not killed, you will bring him back with you, won't you?"

"Yes, we'll be sure to bring him back. We shall be **discharged** in six weeks."

Eddy became a great favorite with the soldiers; and the tall, lank fifer used often to carry him "piggyback" over the hard roads and muddy places.

After the battle of Wilson's Creek, little Eddy could not be found. By and by the corporal, who had been searching for him, heard the sound of his drum not far away.

The company was to march away in a very few minutes, but not liking to leave the little fellow, the corporal went to find him.

He found him sitting up against a tree, looking deadly pale.

"O, Corporal, I am so glad you came! Do give me a drink of water! You don't think I'll die, do you? That man lying there said the doctor would cure my feet."

Poor little Eddy! Both feet had been shot off by a cannon ball. Looking around, the corporal found a Confederate soldier lying dead not far from Eddy. He, poor soldier, although he was himself dying, had crept up to Eddy and tried to bandage the little boy's feet.

While Eddy was telling the story, a Confederate officer came up and took the corporal and his little friend prisoners.

Very tenderly, the officer lifted Eddy upon the horse before him and started for the camp; but before they reached it, the little drummer boy was dead.

Vocabulary

lank: slender; thin

discharged: released from duty

Comprehension Questions

1. How did Eddy persuade the captain to allow him to join their regiment?
2. How did Eddy get injured?
3. What finally happened to Eddy?
4. Currently, one must be 18 years of age, or 17 with parental consent, to enlist in the army. Do you think this is a fair age? Why or why not?

Suggested Reading

The Testimony of Charlie Coulson, by Dr. Max L. Rossvally, Young Men of Valor series. This book tells the true story of a Christian drummer boy during the Civil War.

The Surrender of General Lee

Lawton B. Evans

In April 1865, the Confederate Army, headed by General Robert E. Lee, was surrounded by General Ulysses S. Grant's Union Army. Lee's men were weak and outnumbered, and Lee felt he had no choice but to surrender. The following describes the meeting at which General Lee surrendered to General Grant.

At a house, in the little town of Appomattox, Virginia, on April 9, 1865, a memorable event took place. General Robert E. Lee here met General Ulysses S. Grant and surrendered the Confederate Army under his command.

For four years, the terrible war between the North and South had been going on, until the Southern Army was reduced to a bare handful of ill-fed and badly clothed men. The South had been drained of her men and supplies, and Lee saw it was useless to continue the unequal struggle any longer.

The two great generals met by agreement in this village to arrange terms for the **cessation** of **hostilities**.

The contrast between the two men was striking. Grant was forty-three years of age, five feet, eight inches tall, with brown hair and full brown beard. He wore a single-breasted shirt of dark blue flannel and an ordinary pair of top-boots, with his trousers inside; he was without spurs, and he had no sword. A pair of shoulder straps was all to show his rank. Around him sat or stood a dozen of his staff officers.

Lee, on the other hand, was six feet tall and faultlessly attired. His hair and beard were silver grey, and quite thick for one of his age. He was sixteen years older than Grant. He wore a new Confederate uniform, and, by his side, was a sword of **exquisite** workmanship, the **hilt** studded with jewels. It was the sword presented to him by the State of Virginia. His boots were new and clean, and he wore a pair of handsome spurs. He was attended by a single officer, his military secretary.

Lee was the first to arrive, and, when Grant entered, he arose and bowed **profoundly**. Grant and his officers returned the greeting. Grant then sat at a marble-top table, in the center of the room, while Lee sat at a small oval table, near a window.

General Grant began the conversation by saying, "I met you once before, General Lee, while we were serving in Mexico. I have always remembered your appearance, and I think I should have recognized you anywhere."

"Yes," replied Lee, "I know I met you in Mexico, and I have often thought of it. Those were wonderful experiences for us, when we were young soldiers."

After a few more remarks about Mexico, Lee said, "I suppose, General Grant, that the object of our meeting is understood. I asked to see you to find out upon what terms you would receive the surrender of my army."

Grant replied, "The terms are that all officers and men surrendered are to be paroled, and are not to take up arms again; and all guns, ammunition, and supplies are to be handed over as captured property."

Lee suggested that the terms be written out for his acceptance. This was done, Grant adding that the side arms, horses, and baggage of the officers were not to be included in the terms of surrender. There was no demand made for the surrender of Lee's sword, nor was there any offer of it on Lee's part. In fact, nothing was said about it.

When the document was written, Lee took out his glasses and slowly put them on. Reading the terms of surrender, he remarked, "I would like to mention that the cavalry and artillery own their horses. I would like to know whether those men will be permitted to retain their own stock."

Grant immediately replied, "I take it that most of the men in the ranks are small farmers, and, as the country has been so raided by the armies, it is doubtful if they will be able to put in a crop to carry them through next winter without the aid of the horses they now have. I will instruct the officers to let the men, who claim to own horses or mules, take the animals home with them to work their little farms."

Lee appreciated this **concession** and said, "This will have the very best possible effect upon the men. It will do much toward

conciliating our people." He then wrote out his acceptance of the terms of the surrender.

When this was done, General Grant introduced the members of his staff to General Lee. Some of them Lee had known before, and the conversation became general and **cordial**. Lee at length said, "General Grant, I have a thousand or more of your men as prisoners, a number of them officers. I shall be glad to send them into your lines as soon as possible, for I have no provisions for them. I have indeed nothing for my own men. They have been living for the last few days on parched corn, and we are badly in need of **rations**."

General Grant immediately offered to receive the prisoners back into his own lines and said, "I will take steps to have your army supplied with rations at once." Turning to an officer, he gave the command for the issuing of the rations to the hungry Confederate Army.

The two generals then shook hands, and, bowing gravely to the others, Lee prepared to depart. Reaching the porch, he signaled for the orderly to bring up his horse. When it was ready, he mounted and rode away, to break the sad news to the brave fellows he had so long commanded.

The news of the surrender reached the Union lines, and **firing of salutes** began at several places. Grant sent orders to stop this, saying, "The war is over, and it is ill-becoming to rejoice in the downfall of a gallant foe."

When Lee appeared among his soldiers, they saw by his sad **countenance** that he brought them news of surrender. They stood in silence, as he rode before them, every hat raised, and down the bronzed cheek of thousands of hardened veterans there ran bitter tears.

As Lee rode slowly along the lines, the old soldiers pressed about him, trying to take his hand, to touch his person, or even to lay their hands upon his splendid gray horse, thus showing for him their deep affection. Then General Lee, with bare head, and tears flowing, **bade adieu** to his soldiers. In a few words, he told the brave men, who had been so true, to return to their homes and begin to rebuild their waste lands.

Surrender Terms at Appomattox, 1865

The following are the terms of surrender written at the meeting at Appomattox, Virginia, on April 9, 1865.

General R.E. Lee,
Commanding C.S.A.
APPOMATTOX Ct H., Va.,
April 9,1865,

General;
In accordance with the substance of my letter to you of the 8th inst., I propose to receive the surrender of the Army of Northern Virginia on the following terms, to wit: Rolls of all officers and men to be made in duplicate, one copy to be given to an officer to be designated by me, the other to be retained by such officer or officers as you may designate. The officers to give their individual paroles not to take up arms against the Government of the United States until properly [exchanged], and each company or regimental commander to sign a like parole for the men of their commands. The arms, artillery, and public property to be parked, and stacked, and turned over to the officers appointed by me to receive them. This will not embrace the side-arms of the officers, nor their private horses or baggage. This done, each officer and man will be allowed to return to his home, not to be disturbed by the United States authorities so long as they observe their paroles, and the laws in force where they may reside.

Very respectfully,
U.S. Grant,
Lieutenant-General

Vocabulary

cessation: a final ceasing; a stop

hostilities: fighting

exquisite: flawless; beautiful

hilt: the handle of a sword

profoundly: deeply

concession: something given or granted

conciliating: uniting

cordial: gracious; friendly

rations: food

firing of salutes: the firing of guns in celebration of victory

countenance: look; expression

bade adieu: said good-bye

Comprehension Questions

1. What was the purpose of the meeting between General Lee and General Grant?
2. In your own words, summarize the difference in General Grant's and General Lee's appearances.
3. Name at least two ways the story shows that General Grant was gracious toward General Lee.
4. Most of the story's details of the surrender are accurate, as they come from the writings of General Horace Porter, who attended the meeting. How do the details differ from what you envisioned before you read the story? Did any of the details surprise you?

Extension Activity

Visit the following websites to read more about the surrender of General Robert E. Lee.

⇨ http://www.eyewitnesstohistory.com/appomatx.htm

⇨ http://americancivilwar.com/appo.html

⇨ http://www.sonofthesouth.net/leefoundation/SurrenderatAppomattox.htm

The Blue and the Gray

Francis Miles Finch

On April 25, 1866, a group of ladies decided to decorate the Union and Confederate graves in Columbus, Mississippi, with flowers. When these women were reminded that some of the graves they were decorating were Union soldiers' graves, one of the women remarked, "We are sure there are mothers, sisters, wives, or sweethearts who are mourning these dead men, so we are going to honor them also." This event is credited as the founding of Memorial Day. A poet, Francis Miles Finch, happened to be in town that day and commemorated the occasion with this poem.

By the flow of the inland river,
Whence the fleets of iron have fled,
Where the blades of the grave-grass quiver,
Asleep are the ranks of the dead:
Under the sod and the dew,
Waiting the judgment-day;
Under the one, the Blue,
Under the other, the Gray.

These in the robings of glory,
Those in the gloom of defeat,
All with the battle-blood gory,
In the dusk of eternity meet:
Under the sod and the dew,
Waiting the judgment-day
Under the laurel, the Blue,
Under the willow, the Gray.

From the silence of sorrowful hours
The **desolate** mourners go,
Lovingly laden with flowers
Alike for the friend and the foe;
Under the sod and the dew,
Waiting the judgment-day;
Under the roses, the Blue,
Under the lilies, the Gray.

So with an equal splendor,
The morning sun-rays fall,
With a touch **impartially** tender,
On the blossoms blooming for all:

Under the sod and the dew,
Waiting the judgment-day;
Broidered with gold, the Blue,
Mellowed with gold, the Gray.

So, when the summer calleth,
On forest and field of grain,
With an equal murmur falleth
The cooling drip of the rain:
Under the sod and the dew,
Waiting the judgment day,
Wet with thc rain, the Blue
Wet with the rain, the Gray.

Sadly, but not with **upbraiding**,
The generous deed was done,
In the storm of the years that are fading
No braver battle was won:
Under the sod and the dew,
Waiting the judgment-day;
Under the blossoms, the Blue,
Under the garlands, the Gray.

No more shall the war cry **sever**,
Or the winding rivers be red;
They banish our anger forever
When they laurel the graves of our dead!
Under the sod and the dew,
Waiting the judgment-day,
Love and tears for the Blue,
Tears and love for the Gray.

Vocabulary:

desolate: joyless

impartially: fairly; without favoritism or bias

broidered: embroidered; stitched with needlework

upbraiding: scolding

sever: divide

Unit 6
Important People—Turn of the Century

Booker T. Washington

Patsy Stevens

Born in 1856, Booker T. Washington was a slave who became free and accomplished many things for his fellow African Americans.

Booker T. Washington was born a slave in Franklin County, Virginia. His mother Jane was a cook for the plantation. His mother was black and his father, whom he never knew, was white. He grew up in a small log cabin with a dirt floor. Each night a **pallet** was put on the floor for sleeping. Sometimes to feed her children, Jane would take a chicken or eggs from the master's flock and cook them during the night.

His clothing was made of **flax**, which would prick the skin like needles until the shirt had been worn for about six weeks. Once, his brother John offered to wear Booker's shirt until it was softer. His first pair of shoes had wooden soles and coarse leather tops.

One of his duties as a boy was carrying sacks of corn to the mill on the back of a horse. If a sack fell off, he might wait for hours for someone to come along and replace it on the horse's back.

One day the slaves were all called to the house of their owner, James Burroughs. A paper was read to them telling them they were now free. His step-father, who earlier had gone to West Virginia, sent a wagon to bring Booker and his family to their new home. The trip took about ten days.

After the move, his mother took a young orphan into the family. Now there were four children; James B., who was the new brother, Booker, John, and Amanda.

His step-father, who worked in the salt mines, got jobs for Booker and John in the salt mines. Sometimes they worked in the coal mines.

A man named Mr. William Davis opened a school for black children. Booker's parents permitted him to attend if he worked before and after school. He worked from 4:00 a.m. to 9:00 a.m. in the mines; then went to school half a day. After school he went back to the mines.

He said his first day at school was the happiest day of his life. When the teacher asked his name, he said, "Booker". All the other children gave a first and last name, so Booker chose to take the name "Washington", his step-father's first name, as his second name. He later learned from his mother he did have a second name; Taliaferro.

He soon had to drop out of school to work full time in the coal mine. However, his mother found him another job as a houseboy for the family of General Lewis Ruffner. General Ruffner's wife was very strict with Booker. Once he ran away and started working as a waiter for a steamboat captain, but he didn't know how to be a waiter and failed at the job. He returned to Mrs. Ruffner and she took him back. She arranged for him to get some schooling.

He proved his **trustworthiness** to her by selling fruit and vegetables to the miners and carefully accounting for all the money he received. He found being honest always had its reward. He stayed with Mrs. Ruffner four years and came to regard her as one of the best friends he ever had.

He heard about the Hampton Institute in Virginia, a school for black boys and girls. He was determined to go to the school. In his autobiography, *Up from Slavery*, Washington wrote the following:

> ONE day, while at work in the coal-mine, I happened to overhear two miners talking about a great school for coloured people somewhere in Virginia. This was the first time that I had ever heard anything about any kind of school or college that was more **pretentious** than the little coloured school in our town. In the darkness of the mine I noiselessly crept as close as I could to the two men who were talking. I heard one tell the other that not only was the school established for the members of my race, but that opportunities were provided by which poor but worthy students could work out all or a part of the cost of board, and at the same time be taught some trade or industry. As they went on describing the school, it seemed to me that it must be the greatest place on earth, and not even Heaven presented more attractions for me at that time than did the Hampton Normal and Agricultural Institute in Virginia, about which these men were talking. I **resolved** at once to go to that school, although

> I had no idea where it was, or how many miles away, or how I was going to reach it; I remembered only that I was on fire constantly with one ambition, and that was to go to Hampton. This thought was with me day and night.

He got as far as Richmond, Virginia, and spent a few days there sleeping under a plank sidewalk at night and loading a ship during the day to earn money to buy food.

When he finally arrived at Hampton Institute, the principal told him to sweep a room for her. He knew it was a test. He swept and dusted the room three times until not a speck of dirt remained. He was accepted into the school. He would work as the assistant janitor to pay for his room and board at the school.

Miss Nathalie Lord, one of his teachers at Hampton, gave him lessons in elocution, or public speaking. These lessons would prove **vital** to his success later on.

After graduation he returned to his hometown, Malden, and became a teacher at the first school he ever attended. In the day school he had a class of eighty to ninety students. He also taught night classes and two Sunday school classes. He encouraged several of his students to attend Hampton Institute. He also sent his brother John and his adopted brother James to the school.

General Armstrong, the principal at Hampton, invited Booker to return to the school as a teacher and a post-graduate student. He taught a night class for students who had to work during the day. He also taught a class of seventy-five American Indian boys.

Mr. George Campbell, a prominent white man in Tuskegee, Alabama, wanted to start a school for black children in that town. General Armstrong recommended that Booker open and run the school. The state legislature would give $2000 a year for the school. In 1881, Booker started having classes in an old church and a run-down building. When it rained, one of the taller students would hold an umbrella over the teacher's head to keep him dry.

Finally, he was able to purchase farmland eventually totaling over 2,000 acres on which to build the school.

He married Fannie Smith and they had a daughter, Portia. Within the year Fannie passed away and did not get to see Portia grow up nor see the school succeed.

All students at the school were required to work in addition to their academic studies. They chopped trees, cleared land, made bricks, built furniture, and constructed buildings. Classes were started to teach trades and professions. The following explains how students made their own furniture and were taught to revere cleanliness:

> It was my aim from the first at Tuskegee to not only have the buildings **erected** by the students themselves, but to have them make their own furniture as far as was possible. I now **marvel** at the patience of the students while sleeping upon the floor while waiting for some kind of a **bedstead** to be constructed, or at their sleeping without any kind of a mattress while waiting for something that looked like a mattress to be made.
>
> In the early days we had very few students who had been used to handling carpenter's tools, and the bedsteads made by the students then were very rough and very weak. Not unfrequently when I went into the students' rooms in the morning I would find at least two bedsteads lying about on the floor. The problem of providing mattresses was a difficult one to solve. We finally mastered this, however, by getting some cheap cloth and sewing pieces of this together so as to make large bags. These bags we filled with the pine straw—or, as it is sometimes called, pine needles—which we secured from the forests nearby. I am glad to say that the industry of mattress-making has grown steadily since then, and has been improved to such an extent that at the present time it is an important branch of the work which is taught **systematically** to a number of our girls, and that the mattresses that now come out of the mattress-shop at Tuskegee are about as good as those bought in the average store. For some time after the opening of the boarding department we had no chairs in the students' bedrooms or in the dining rooms. Instead of chairs we used stools which the students constructed by nailing together three pieces of rough board. As a

> rule, the furniture in the students' rooms during the early days of the school consisted of a bed, some stools, and sometimes a rough table made by the students. The plan of having the students make the furniture is still followed, but the number of pieces in a room has been increased, and the **workmanship** has so improved that little fault can be found with the articles now. One thing that I have always insisted upon at Tuskegee is that everywhere there should be absolute cleanliness. Over and over again the students were reminded in those first years—and are reminded now—that people would excuse us for our poverty, for our lack of comforts and conveniences, but that they would not excuse us for dirt.

Booker T. Washington was an **eloquent** speaker and used this skill for the benefit of Tuskegee Institute. The school continued to grow.

Soon, Booker married again. Olivia Davidson, assistant principal of the school, was his wife for four years and mother to two sons before she too passed away. Four years later he married Maggie Murray, a teacher at Tuskegee.

In 1895 he was invited to give a speech at an **exposition** in Atlanta. The exposition was designed to promote the southern region to the world and encourage trade with Latin America. In his speech, Booker urged blacks and whites to work together. Afterward, Harvard University gave him an **honorary** degree.

Friends gave money for Booker and his wife to visit Europe, where they had tea with Queen Victoria.

The school flourished. George Washington Carver came to teach **agricultural** science. People of wealth took an interest in the education of blacks. Andrew Carnegie, who made his fortune in the steel industry and became "the richest man in the world," helped.

Booker T. Washington, more than any other black man of his time, helped to **elevate** his people through education.

I pity the man, black or white, who has never experienced the joy and satisfaction that come to one by reason of an effort to assist in making someone else more useful and more happy.

—Booker T. Washington

Vocabulary

pallet: a straw-filled mattress

flax: a plant from which linen is made

trustworthiness: the quality of being deserving of trust or confidence

pretentious: appearing important or valuable

resolved: decided

vital: necessary; important

erected: built; assembled

marvel: to become filled with surprise

bedstead: the framework of a bed

systematically: regularly, as if on a schedule

workmanship: the quality of a piece of work

eloquent: having clear and forceful expression

exposition: a public exhibition

honorary: given as a sign of honor

agricultural: having to do with farming

elevate: to lift up or make higher; raise

Comprehension Questions

1. Describe at least two aspects of Booker's life as the son of a slave.
2. Under what conditions did his parents allow Booker to attend Mr. Davis's school?
3. How did he get the last name of "Washington"?
4. How did he prove himself to the principal at Hampton School?
5. What did the students at Tuskegee Institute do besides study their lessons?
6. In your opinion, why is Booker T. Washington seen as an important historical figure?

Extension Activity

Complete the crossword puzzle on page 12 of the Student Exercises *booklet.*

The Great War Chief Joseph of the Nez Percés

Oliver Otis Howard

"If the white man wants to live in peace with the Indian, he can live in peace. Treat all men alike. Give them a chance to live and grow."—Chief Joseph

In 1877, General Oliver Otis Howard was commanded to meet with Chief Joseph of the Nez Percés (meaning pierced noses) tribe in Idaho to settle a dispute about a land treaty. The following account, told by Howard himself, describes the encounter, as well as the men's interesting and lengthy relationship.

I agreed to meet Joseph and his friends at Lapwai, Idaho, and we all hoped that the meeting would result in a good peace. When I arrived at Fort Lapwai, an immense tent was ready for the **council**. Joseph, with about fifty Indians, had spent the night nearby in handsome Indian lodges. His many ponies, watched by Indian lads, were feeding on the banks of Lapwai Creek. All was excitement, as with some officers I waited for the Indians to come that sunny morning to the "big talk." At last they came, riding slowly up the grass, Joseph and his brother Ollicut riding side by side. The faces of all the Indians were painted bright red, the paint covering the partings of the hair, the braids of the warriors' hair tied with strips of white and scarlet. No weapons were in sight except tomahawk-pipes and sheath-knives in their belts. Everything was **ornamented** with beads. The women wore bright-colored shawls and skirts of cotton to the top of their moccasins.

They all came up and formed a line facing us; then they began a song. The song was wild and shrill and fierce, yet so **plaintive** at times it was almost like weeping, and made us sorry for them. However, we were glad that there were fifty instead of 500.

They turned off to the right and swept around outside our fence, keeping up the strange song all the way around the fort, where it broke up into irregular bubblings, like mountain streams tumbling over stones.

Then the women and children rode away at a gallop and the braves, leaving their ponies, came in a single file with Joseph ahead. They passed us, each one formally shaking hands, and then we all sat down in the big tent. After a prayer, I spoke to Joseph and told him that his brother Ollicut had said to me twelve days ago in Walla Walla that he wished to see me—now I was ready to listen to what he wished to say. Joseph then said that more Indians were coming; they were to be here soon and we must not be in a hurry, but wait for them. So we put off the "big talk" till the next day.

Again the Indians went through the same performance, and again we were ready. White Bird, the leader of another small Nez Percés tribe, had arrived. With a white eagle wing in his hand, he sat beside Joseph. Joseph introduced him to me, saying, "This is White Bird; it is the first time he has seen you." There was also an old chief, Too-hul-hul-sote, who hated white men. When they were seated again, I told them that the President wanted them all to come up to Lapwai, to the part where nobody lived, and take up the **vacant reservation**, for the other lands had been given to the white men.

Joseph said, "Too-hul-hul-sote will speak."

The old man was very angry and said, "What person pretends to divide the land and put me on it?"

I answered, "I am the man."

Then among the Indians all about me signs of anger began to appear. Looking-Glass dropped his gentle style and made rough answers. White Bird, hiding his face behind that eagle wing, said he had not been brought up to be governed by white men; and Joseph began to finger his tomahawk, and his eyes flashed.

Too-hul-hul-sote said fiercely, "The others may do as they like; I am not going on that land."

Then I spoke to them. I told them I was going to look at the vacant land, and they should come with me. The old man, Too-hul-hul-sote, should stay at the fort with the colonel till we came back.

He arose and cried, "Do you want to frighten me about my body?"

But I said, "I will leave you with the colonel," and at a word a soldier led the brave old fellow out of the tent and gave him to a guard.

Then Joseph quieted the Indians and agreed to go with me. We did not **hasten** our ride, but started after a few days. We then rode over forty miles together.

Once Joseph said to me, "If we come and live here, what will you give us—schools, teachers, houses, churches, and gardens?"

I said, "Yes."

"Well!" said Joseph, "those are just the things we do not want. The earth is our mother, and do you think we want to dig and break it? No, indeed! We want to hunt buffalo and fish for salmon, not plow and use the hoe."

"Yours is a strange answer," I said. After riding all over the country, the Indians called it a good country, and they agreed to come and live there. The land was staked out, and Too-hul-hul-sote set free. It was arranged that in thirty days all the outside Indians should be on the reservation, and we parted the best of friends.

Now, about this time Joseph's wife was taken sick, so he left his band and stayed away some distance with her in his lodge. While he was away, some of the young warriors came to a farmhouse and began to talk with two white men. For some reason, they did not agree, and a young Indian tried to take a gun out of the farmer's hand. At once the farmer was frightened and called to the other white man for help. That white man ran up and began to shoot, killing the Indian. Now began all sorts of trouble. The Indians stole horses, burned houses, and robbed travelers; and the whole country was wild with terror.

Joseph at first did not know what to do, but at last he broke his agreement with me and all the outside Indians went on the warpath. For many months there were battles—battles—battles! Joseph was a splendid warrior, and with many of Uncle Sam's good soldiers he fought.

I followed him for over 1,400 miles, over mountains and valleys, always trying to make him give up. At the last I sent two Nez Percé friends, "Captain John" and "Indian George" to Chief

Joseph's strong place in the Little Rockies with a white flag to ask him to give up.

Joseph sent back word: "I have done all I can; I now trust my people and myself to your mercy."

So the surrender was arranged, and just before night on October 5, 1877, Joseph, followed by his people, many of whom were lame and wounded, came up to me and offered his rifle.

Beside me stood General N. A. Miles, who had helped me and fought the last battle, and so I told Joseph that he, General Miles, would take the rifle for me.

Thus ended the great Nez Percé War, and Joseph went after a time to live with Moses, another chief of whom I will tell you some day.

Twenty-seven years later I met Chief Joseph, the greatest Indian warrior I ever fought with, at the Carlisle Indian School, and there he made a speech: "For a long time," he said, "I did want to kill General Howard, but now I am glad to meet him and we are friends!"

> *Tell General Howard I know his heart. What he told me before, I have it in my heart. I am tired of fighting. Our chiefs are killed; Looking Glass is dead; Ta-Hool-Hool-Shute is dead. The old men are all dead; it is the young men who say yes or no. He who led on the young men is dead. It is cold, and we have no blankets; the little children are freezing to death. My people, some of them, have run away to the hills and have no blankets, no food. No one knows where they are—perhaps freezing to death. I want to have time to look for my children, and see how many of them I can find. Maybe I shall find them among the dead. Hear me, my chiefs! I am tired; my heart is sick and sad. From where the sun now stands I will fight no more forever.*
>
> —Surrender Speech, Chief Joseph, October 5, 1877

Vocabulary

council: meeting

ornamented: decorated

plaintive: mournful; expressing suffering or woe

vacant: empty

reservation: a piece of land set aside for use by American Indians

hasten: move or act quickly

Comprehension Questions

1. What news did General Howard bring to Chief Joseph of the Nez Percés?
2. How did Chief Joseph respond when General Howard said the white men would give them schools, teachers, houses, churches, and gardens?
3. Although an agreement was reached, battles soon broke out. Why?
4. How and when did the fighting finally come to an end?
5. By the end of the story, how do the two men regard each other?

Extension Activity

Complete the sequencing worksheet on page 13 of the Student Exercises *booklet.*

Dr. Eleanor Chesnut:

Missionary Martyr of Lien Chou China

Julia H. Johnston

As a child, Dr. Eleanor Chesnut experienced hardship; however, she never indulged in self-pity. Read to find out how Dr. Chesnut overcame obstacles and greatly impacted China for Christ.

You cannot know, as you read, how hard it is to write of this dear, personal friend, once a visitor in the home, and bound to the heart by the tenderest ties. But it is such a lasting joy to have known her that the story must have a **jubilant** note in it, all through, as it tells of her wonderfully heroic life and martyr crown. You need not be afraid to read it, for it should make you glad that such a brave soul ever lived her life of sacrifice and service.

It had a very pitiful beginning—this life we are thinking about now. It began in the town of Waterloo, Iowa, on January 8, 1868. Just after Eleanor's birth, her father disappeared mysteriously and was never again heard of. The mother, who had the respect and sympathy of her neighbors, died not long after, and the family, consisting of several brothers and sisters, was **scattered**.

Eleanor, who was but three at the time, was adopted, though not legally, by some friendly people near, who had no children. They had little money, but did the best they could for her, finding her a puzzle and a comfort both. In later years the father spoke of her "loving, kindly ways, her obedience in the family circle, and her unselfishness."

But the poor child was not happy. She was lonesome and longed for mother-love. Well as she controlled her feelings, she did not like to be **restrained**, and often carried a stormy little heart within. She was happiest when in school, but when only twelve, she was distressed to find that she might have to give up study altogether. It was then that she went to live with an aunt in Missouri, in a "backwoods" country, where school privileges were of the poorest. And besides, the struggle for life was too hard to allow a chance to study or spare anything for the expense of schooling.

The news of Park College, Parkville, Missouri, where students had a chance to earn their way, at least in part, came in some roundabout manner, and from that moment the girl made up her mind that she would go, come what might. And go she did, through the kind encouragement of the president of the college. She entered, feeling **forlorn** and friendless, but soon found warm friends and **congenial** surroundings. Her studies were a continual delight. But how to live was a problem. Her family could do little for her, and she had to take the **bounty** of missionary boxes when it came to clothing. It was such a struggle to accept these supplies that she could not feel very grateful in her sensitive heart, but it was really heroic to wear the things. Don't you think so?

These hard trials in youth had "peaceable fruits" afterwards, for they ripened into a wonderful gentleness, sympathy, tact, and understanding, which made her a blessing to others. Writing to a friend, in later years, about the poor boys in China needing clothes, she said, "The poor boys! They are so shabby that I wish I could do more for them. I remember how shabby I was at Park College years ago. I do not mind nearly so much now, wearing old things."

Outwardly the student was brave and quiet, but there was a **tumult** within that was only hushed when she became a Christian. Afterwards came the determination to become a missionary. She said a pathetic thing about this decision. (How it comes back in her very tones this moment!) She said, "One thing that made me feel that I ought to go was the fact that there was really no one to mind very much if I did." But this was not said in a **dismal**, self-pitying way. The larger reason she gave at another time and place, when asked for it in connection with her appointment. She said simply that it was "a desire to do good in what seemed the most fitting sphere."

In 1888, on leaving Park College, the young girl entered upon the study of medicine. She had no great natural love for the profession, but, as she confided, it seemed as if it would add so much to her usefulness. She said that it was very hard the first year, and she wondered if she could go on and finish the course, but she resolved that she would. And she did, with a **resolute** will, even becoming interested in it, as she plunged heart and mind into the study that she was sure would make her more helpful. But a missionary friend, who knew her well in Lien Chou, said afterwards that this girl should have been an artist, not a doctor, if her real nature had been consulted, and that it was perfectly heroic in her to practice medicine and surgery as she did.

The medical course was taken in Chicago, with the advantage of a scholarship, but the student "lived in an attic, cooked her own meals, and almost starved," as a Chicago friend afterwards insisted. Her meals were principally oatmeal. A course in the Illinois Training School for Nurses in Chicago followed, and some money was earned by nursing in times allotted for vacations. She served as nurse to **Dr. Oliver Wendell Holmes** in his final illness. The training was made more complete by a winter in an institution in Massachusetts, and then came a course of Bible training in Moody Institute, Chicago.

In 1893 Dr. Chesnut was appointed as medical missionary to the foreign field, and was assigned to China. She had a strange, natural **aversion** to the water, but was a brave sailor notwithstanding. After a little time at Sam Kong, studying the language and doing some **incidental** work, the doctor was appointed to Lien Chou. From a letter in print this extract is taken. (You can see that she was "a saint with a sense of humor," bless her! There was some good Irish blood in her, which no doubt gave the twinkle in her brown eyes.)

> Here I am at last. I had a few things carried overland. The boats are on their way. They have divided their cargoes with several others and are floating the hospital bed-boards and my springs. Won't they be rusty? I only hope they won't try to float the books and the organ. I don't mind being alone here at all. ... I have to perform all my operations in my bathroom, which was as small as the law allowed before. Now, with an operating table, it is decidedly full. But I do not mind these inconveniences at all. ... A druggist gave me a prescription which you may find useful, though the ingredients may be more difficult to **procure** in America than in China. You catch some little rats before they get their eyes open, pound to a jelly, and add lime and peanut oil. Warranted to cure any kind of an ulcer.

A missionary from Lien Chou lately told how Dr. Chesnut began the building of a hospital.

When her monthly salary payment came, she saved out $1.50 for her living, and with the rest bought bricks. At last the Missions Board in New York found this out and insisted upon paying back what she had spent on bricks for the hospital. She refused to take the whole sum, saying that to do it, would "spoil all her fun."

The story of the **amputation** of a Chinese **coolie's** leg without any surgical assistance has gone far and wide. The operation was successful, but the flaps of skin did not unite as the doctor hoped, and she knew that any failure in getting well would be resented by the people and perhaps result in a mob. By and by the man recovered perfectly, and, later, the doctor secured some crutches for him from America. But, at the time, it was noticed that Dr. Chesnut was limping. There was no use in asking her why, for the slightest hint brought out the words, "Oh, it's nothing." But one of the women betrayed the truth. The doctor had taken skin from her own leg to transplant upon what the woman called "that good-for-nothing coolie," and had done it without an **anesthetic**, except probably a local application, transferring it at once to the patient. What do you think of heroism like that? And then to say nothing about it!

When the **Boxer troubles** sent foreigners to the coast for safety, Dr. Chesnut refused to go for some months, and went at last under pressure from others, not from fear. She returned in the spring. That same season she came home on **furlough**, when "none knew her but to love her." A tour among societies supporting a ward in Lien Chou Hospital endeared her to many. She was so bright, so engaging, so interesting, and withal showing a sweet humility most touching. At this time she had the first silk dress ever owned. It must have been given to her!

Returning to her work for two busy, blessed years, there came the October day in 1905 when a **mob**, excited and bent on trouble, attacked the hospital. Dr. Chesnut, coming upon the scene, hurried to report to the authorities, and might have escaped, but returned to see if she could help others, and met her cruel death at the hands of those she would have saved. Her last act was to tear strips from her dress to bandage a wound she discovered in the forehead of a boy in the crowd. The crown of martyrdom was then placed upon her own head.

"She being dead, yet speaketh." The same day she died, the Presbyterian Foreign Mission Board received a letter from Dr. Chesnut, written weeks earlier; in it she wrote a poem concerning her own questions about divine guidance. It shows her desire for an understanding of God's will in her life.

The True, Safe Way

by Eleanor Chesnut

Being in doubt, I say
Lord, make it plain!
Which is the true, safe way?
Which would be in vain?

I am not wise to know,
Not sure of foot to go,
My blind eyes cannot see
What is so clear to Thee;
Lord, make it clear to me.

Being perplexed, I say,
Lord, make it right!
Night is as day to Thee,
Darkness as light.

I am afraid to touch
Things that involve so much;
My trembling hand may shake,

My skilless hand may break—
Thine can make no mistake.

Vocabulary

jubilant: filled with great joy

scattered: separated; put in different places

restrained: held back from doing or expressing something

forlorn: sad and lonely

congenial: pleasant

bounty: generous gift

tumult: confusion

dismal: depressing

resolute: bold and faithful

Dr. Oliver Wendell Holmes: a famous doctor and writer

aversion: a dislike

incidental: not very important

procure: obtain; get

amputation: an operation in which a limb of the body is removed

coolie: a worker

anesthetic: a substance that allows the body not to feel pain

Boxer troubles: troubles associated with a group of Chinese rebels, known as Boxers, who did not want missionaries in their country

furlough: a leave of absence from duty granted

mob: an angry group of people

Comprehension Questions

1. Describe at least two of the hardships Dr. Chesnut endured as a child.
2. How did these hardships affect Dr. Chesnut's character and personality?
3. Describe at least one extraordinary act that Dr. Chesnut performed as a missionary in China.
4. Briefly describe Dr. Chesnut's death.
5. Name at least two lessons readers can learn from reading the story of Dr. Chesnut's life.

Extension Activity

Fill out the Understanding Character Traits activity on page 14 of the Student Exercises *booklet.*

Adoniram Judson: Missionary to Burma

Julia H. Johnston

Adoniram Judson led a fascinating and sometimes frustrating life as a missionary to the country of Burma, now known as Myanmar. This biography details his extraordinary life.

A dark-eyed baby boy lay in his old-fashioned cradle about 200 years ago. In the little town of Malden, Massachusetts, August 9, 1788, this child was born and named Adoniram, after his father, who was Reverend Adoniram Judson, a **Congregational** minister in that far-away time. The father, and the mother, too, thought this baby was a wonderful child and determined that he should do a great deal of good in the world. They thought that the best way to get him ready for a great work was to begin early to teach him as much as he could possibly learn. Long pieces were given him to commit to memory when he was hardly more than a baby, and he learned to read when he was three. Think of it!

When he was four, he liked best of all to gather all the children in the neighborhood about him and play church. He always preached the sermon himself, and his favorite hymn was, "Go, Preach My Gospel, Saith the Lord." This was a good way to have a happy time, and he wasn't a bit too young to think about telling others the Good News, for he was old enough to know about Jesus and His love.

The little Adoniram, like boys who live now, liked to find out about things himself. When he was seven, he thought he would see if the sun moved. For a long time he lay flat on his back in the morning sunlight, looking up to the sky through a hole in his hat. He was away from home so long that he was missed, and his sister discovered him, with his swollen eyes nearly blinded by the light. He told her that he had "found out about the sun's moving," but did not explain how he knew.

At ten this boy studied Latin and Greek, and at sixteen he went to Brown University, from which he was graduated, as **valedictorian** of his class, when he was nineteen. He was a great student, loving study, and ambitious to do and be something very grand and great indeed. Two years after this, he became a Christian; and then came a great longing to be a minister, and he studied diligently with this end in view. There was one question that this splendid young man asked about everything, and this was, "Is it pleasing to God?" He put this question in several places in his room so that he would be sure to see and remember it.

Mr. Judson taught school for a while, wrote some schoolbooks, and traveled about to see the world. After some years he read a little book called *The Star in the East*. It was a missionary book, and it turned the young man's thoughts to missions. At last he seemed to hear a voice saying, "Go ye," and with all his heart he said, "I will go." From that moment he never once **faltered** in his determination to be a missionary. His thoughts turned towards **Burma**, and he longed to go there. About this time Mr. Judson met four young men who had held a prayer-meeting in the rain. They had sheltered themselves in a haystack, and there promised God to serve Him as missionaries if He would send them out. These five were of one heart, and were much together encouraging one another. There was no money to send out missionaries, and Mr. Judson was sent to London to see if the Society there would promise some support.

The ship was captured by a **privateer**, and the young man was made prisoner, but he found an American who got him out of the filthy cell. This man came in, wearing a large cloak, and was allowed to go into the cell to see if he knew any of the prisoners. When he came to Mr. Judson, he threw his cape over him, hiding him from the jailer, and got him out safely. He gave him a piece of money and sent him on his way.

The London Society was not ready to take up the support of American missionaries, but not long after this, the American Board, in Boston, sent him to Burma, with his lovely young bride, whose name, as a girl, was Ann Hasseltine. It took a year and a half to reach the **field** in Rangoon, Burma, and get finally settled, in a poor, forlorn house, ready to study the language. By this time, Mr. Judson was taken under the care of the Baptist Board, just organized, as he felt that he belonged there. Most Burmans were **Buddhists**, and the fierce governors of the people were called "**Eaters**." The work was very hard, but the missionary said that the **prospects** were "bright as the promises of God." When he was thirty-one and had been in Burma six years, he baptized the first convert to Christianity.

The preparation of a dictionary, and the translation of the New Testament, now occupied much time.

After this came great trouble. It was wartime. Missionaries were unwelcome. Dr. Judson was put in a dreadful prison. His wife was able to hide his translation of the New Testament in a case disguised as a pillow and smuggle it in to him. After great suffering there, his wife pleaded with guards to allow him to stay in an empty lion's cage because he was critically ill with fever. He was able to stay there for three weeks. After he left the prison, a servant of Dr. Judson's found and preserved the precious translation of the New Testament. Set free at last, he went on with his work.

Death came to his home again and again, and trials bitter to bear. For thirty-seven years he toiled on, several times returning to America, but hastening back to his field. By that time there were sixty-three churches in Burma, under the care of 163 missionaries and helpers, and over 7,000 converts had been baptized. Worn out with long labor, the hero-missionary, stricken again with fever, was sent home, only to die on shipboard, and his body was buried at sea.

Vocabulary

Congregational: A Protestant Christian denomination

valedictorian: the student usually having the highest rank in a graduating class

faltered: hesitated in purpose or drive

Burma: a country in southeastern Asia, also known as Myanmar

privateer: an armed private ship, in this case from France, permitted by its government to make war on ships of an enemy country

field: place where a missionary serves God

Buddhists: people of a religion of eastern and central Asia growing out of the teaching of Gautama Buddha

Eaters: a nickname given to the governors because they would overtax the Burmese people

prospects: possibilities

Comprehension Questions

1. What was Adoniram's favorite activity when he was four years old?
2. In what country did Adoniram Judson serve as a missionary? What religion were most of the people?
3. Why was Reverend Judson put in prison?
4. What lasting effects did Reverend Judson have on Burma?
5. Describe Reverend Judson's death and burial.

Extension Activity

Reverend Judson's wife Ann was also an extraordinary person. Visit the following website to learn more about her:

⇨ http://www.christianity.com/church/church-history/timeline/1801-1900/ann-judson-1st-american-woman-missionary-11630365.html

Write a paragraph containing the most important facts you learn.

Unit 7
The Life of the Cowboy

The Cowboy

Lawton B. Evans

Have you ever wondered what it would be like to be a cowboy? Read on to find out!

No inhabitant of the West is more revered than the cowboy. We have all seen his picture and read of his exploits in the early days when cattle roamed wild and free over the western plains, and the cowboy went in search of employment and adventure. He was generally young, strong, and ready to undergo any hardship and endure any **privation**. He could sleep on the plains, endure heat and cold, and never grow tired as long as he was in the saddle and underneath him was a good pony.

He dressed as a cowboy should, a thick shirt and heavy trousers, his legs protected by sheepskin flaps to keep off the thorns and thistles from the bushes and the tall grass. He wore a tall, soft **sombrero** with broad brim slouched down over his heavy mat of hair and half **concealing** his smiling, good-natured face. He wore a hunting shirt and sometimes a bright necktie for the sake of color. Around his waist there was a belt containing **cartridges** and a holster that held his ready **six-shooter**. He was an unfailing shot and could draw his gun and shoot so quick that the eye could hardly follow his hand. And yet he was kind and generous and never shot except in self-defense or in the protection of what he considered to be his rights and property. One was always safe in the hands of the cowboy except when trying to cheat or steal. Then justice was swift and sure, and life was in the hands of him who could draw the first gun.

The cowboy got his pony from the wild herds that roamed the plains. These wild ponies had come from those that the Mexicans had driven up from Mexico or that the Indians themselves had **procured** and turned loose on the plains. These herds **accumulated** from year to year, until at one time the wild horses and ponies were very numerous. The cowboys would **pursue** these herds of wild horses, select a likely one from the herd, rope him and tie him and brand him, and then proceed to tame him and make of him a good cow pony. These cow ponies were wiry and strong and could go for miles without tiring and could live on almost nothing. The cowboy and his pony became inseparable. They knew each other by sight and sound, and no matter how late the cowboy might stay during one of his nights in town, the pony always waited for him and would be ready to carry him back to the ranch house.

The duty of the cowboy was to look after the cattle. It was his business to see that the herd did not wander or get separated. He had to ride around them time and time again to see that there were no strays and that no cattle thief could steal them, and that no wolves could attempt to take off the **yearlings**. The larger the herd, the more cowboys were needed. Sometimes when the herd stampeded, these knights of the prairies would ride headlong, hour after hour, so that the herd might not be scattered or lost in the hills.

It was the cowboy's business to rope the cattle at the time of the rodeo and attend to the branding. He had to herd and drive the market cattle sometimes hundreds of miles to a distant port or market where they were sold into Mexico or to the trading vessels or to the larger towns of the border. Then it was his business to see that the money was brought back to his master. And he always performed his duties with unvaried faithfulness.

His main reliance was the swiftness of his pony and his ever ready six-shooter. In the early days there was almost no law out on the plains, and every man was his own protector. He did not take time to appeal to any court but had to take the law in his own hands whenever his life was in danger or whenever a cattle thief or a horse thief was identified.

The greatest crime of the plains was to steal a horse. One might as well steal a member of the family and try to get away with it as to steal a cowboy's pony. The horse thief was despised and pursued and hanged to the nearest tree when he was caught. It was bad enough to be a cattle thief, but to be a horse thief was to bring down the **vengeance** of every cowboy who knew about it and swift **retribution** from the owner of the stolen horse.

The cowboy had his faults, of course. When he was paid off or the roundup was over and the cattle sold, then he and his companions would take themselves to the nearest town where there were gambling and drinking and merry days and nights. Being on the plains for many months, bunking in the ranch house with no others except his own companions and the thousands of cattle around him, and having no sight or sound of anything that could amuse him was **intolerable**; therefore, he let himself loose when his days of vacation came. Sometimes he rode into town firing his pistol and calling for a drink at every bar.

Oftentimes the cowboys would shoot up the town. Not that they would kill anybody—but just for the fun of shooting their pistols and making a noise and scaring everybody and pretending that they were dangerous. They would make the night hideous. Often they would spend the season's earnings in a few weeks of **debauchery**. They would buy the best saddles they could find, gamble away all their money in the gambling halls, and drink all the whiskey that they could; and all this regardless of expense. So long as he had money he was willing to spend it, and he bought whatever he liked.

And this is the reason why we thrill when we read stories of the deeds of daring of the cowboys who tended the vast herds upon the Great Plains of the West.

Vocabulary

privation: the state of being deprived

sombrero: a tall hat with a very wide brim worn especially in the Southwest and Mexico

concealing: hiding

cartridge: a tube containing a complete charge for a firearm

six-shooter: a revolver with six chambers

procured: gotten possession of

accumulated: increased in number

pursue: to follow in order to catch up with and seize

yearlings: horses that are a year old or in the second year after birth

vengeance: punishment given in return for an offense

retribution: something given in payment for a wrong

intolerable: unbearable

debauchery: acts involving extreme and unreasonable involvement in physical pleasures

Comprehension Questions

1. List three admirable qualities of the cowboy. Then list two faults.
2. Where did a cowboy get his pony?
3. Explain the cowboy's main duties.
4. Why was it so important that a cowboy's pony was swift?
5. What would happen if a person was caught stealing a horse?

Extension Activity

Peruse the following websites to learn more about cowboys:

- ⇨ http://hubpages.com/education/Top-Ten-Facts-About-the-Wild-West-and-Cowboys
- ⇨ http://www.history.com/topics/cowboys
- ⇨ https://web.archive.org/web/20120915115647/http://span.state.gov/wwwfspjanfeb0730.pdf

The Last Ride

Christopher Scott

This touching story describes the strong bond that forms between a cowboy and his horse.

Owen Edwards slowly led his injured horse toward home. The big **roan** was favoring its left front leg again. This was the third time in the past year Owen had to walk back to the house, but this time was different, as the pace was much slower and more solemn. Owen knew this day would come, but he dreaded it just the same. The situation was forcing him to make a decision he had been putting off for some time now. The slow pace gave him ample time to think over all his options once again.

They never changed. The only difference this time around was that, this time, he actually had to choose one.

It's not like he was caught off guard. He had been preparing for this very day since last spring when he purchased a yearling colt from his neighbors at the Bar M just down the road, a handsome little **buckskin** that had caught his eye. He had worked with the **colt** through the summer, **breaking** it and getting it accustomed to the feel of a saddle and a **bit**.

But no matter how much Owen knew the truth of it, the reality of the situation was that he just couldn't find the courage within himself to give up on his trusted **steed** altogether. He really knew better than to think all would be well, especially after the second time this had happened. And now here he was once again, "**riding shank's mare**" with a **lame** horse.

He blamed himself for being so hardheaded, but the bond between the two was proving itself to be a difficult thing to break, and it was tearing him apart.

His horse, Grayson, had been his faithful friend and constant companion for over twelve years now. They had been together during good times and bad, and not once had Grayson ever let him down. During the worst of days, he hung tough with Owen, never wavering, never faltering, and always ready to do whatever was asked of him. Grayson would swim swollen rivers, climb steep grades, and maneuver along some of the narrowest cliffside trails in the state of New Mexico without a flinch or a second's hesitation.

Today had proved itself to be a bad day for both Grayson and Owen. Today's injury was a bad ending to a gallant effort to get him over the hump with this leg issue. But the effort went way beyond hope and in all reality shouldn't have even been tried a second time. So now it had come down to this. Today Owen was being forced to make the **inevitable** decision concerning the fate of his horse. Difficult? Yes, but it could no longer be postponed.

He couldn't begin to imagine how things would be without the big roan. They had been inseparable for all these years.

As they slowly walked along, Owen yearned to reset the clock, to turn back the hands of time and start again. But deep down, he knew the thought was nothing more than a feeble attempt to prolong the inevitable.

As they crested the last small rise, Owen could see the ranch ahead. The journey's end was in sight, and before long, Owen was soon walking Grayson into the dimly lit barn. Stopping in front of Grayson's stall, he dropped the reigns to the ground. And with a heavy heart and tears in his eyes he turned toward Grayson and rubbed his warm, soft nose. The horse returned the affection by nuzzling up against Owen's chest. The two stood close for as long as time would allow. Instinctively, each one felt the other's pain. But for now, there was nothing either one of them could do but stand silently and console each other.

Owen eventually moved to Grayson's side and gently lifted the injured leg to get a closer look. Again, the once torn ligaments had not healed correctly. The leg was badly swollen and painful. Owen set the leg down easy and unbuckled the **cinch**. He slowly pulled the saddle off Grayson's back and hung it over the **tack rail**.

As he grabbed hold of the saddle blanket, his mind wandered back to the time when he had first set eyes on Grayson. He was all of fourteen, and his father had gone into town to pick up a few supplies. Owen had stayed behind, tending to a few minor chores around the ranch. He was behind the main house stacking firewood when his father returned.

"Owen!" he called. "Come out to the barn for a minute. I need you to give me a hand with something."

Owen made his way to the barn and was met by the smiling faces of his parents as they stood in the center of the barn with a young roan colt standing between them. The colt was tall and lean, and his color was a mixture of **bay** and gray.

"Happy Birthday, Owen!" shouted his parents. "He needs to be broke, but he's all yours," added his father. "You know, Owen, sometimes your Ma and I don't always show our appreciation like we should, but we surely do want you to know just how much we love you and appreciate all the hard work you put in around this place. The Good Lord could not have blessed us with a better son than you, Owen. And to show our appreciation, your mother and I figured it was about time you had a horse of your own… Oh, yes, before I forget, there is one more thing."

And with that, Owen's mother promptly produced a new saddle blanket from behind her back and handed it to Owen.

It was a handsome-looking quilted blanket, made from a heavy wool fabric with a colorful pattern running through it.

"Your mother made it herself," bragged Owen's father. "Best lookin' saddle blanket I've ever seen."

Owen couldn't have agreed more as he thanked his parents for such wonderful gifts. He named the horse Grayson. It was the beginning of a beautiful friendship between a man and his steed.

These days the blanket's colors were a bit faded, and it was showing signs of wear in a few spots, but it still had plenty of life left in it and would continue to bring a fair amount of comfort to the new horse. A good saddle blanket was a welcome **buffer** between a horse and the harsh reality of hard leather. It helped keep the daily **rigors** of a long trail bearable.

Owen removed the blanket from Grayson's back and draped it over the tack rail next to the saddle. He led the limping horse into its stall and, after removing the bridle, he tended to the sore leg. Strong **liniment** and a tight wrap would do for now. Owen rubbed him down, then fed and watered him. Once Grayson had been taken care of, he reluctantly and slowly made his way back up to the house. Owen knew the prudent thing to do would be to put the animal down, but then Owen wasn't always a prudent man. He could no more put Grayson down than a man could put down one of his own children. Owen had made his decision. He would tend to Grayson's injury and, if all went well, he would retire him to the north pasture, allowing him to live out his days enjoying the warmth of the noonday sun and chewing sweet grass to his heart's content. It was the least he could do for the friend who had been so faithful to him all these years.

As Owen settled in for the evening, he felt a sense of relief. He knew he had made the right decision concerning Grayson, but it would still take a few days before he came to terms with the fact that he would no longer be riding him. It was hard to believe that today was their last ride.

Tomorrow he would throw the old saddle blanket upon the back of his new horse. Tomorrow, thought Owen, he would begin in earnest to build a new friendship. It was time for the young horse, which he had named Cimarron, to begin earning his keep.

Vocabulary

roan: a dark color sprinkled with white

buckskin: a horse of a dull yellowish color with black mane and tail

colt: a young male horse

breaking: taming a horse

bit: the usually metal bar attached to a bridle and put in the mouth of a horse

steed: a lively horse

riding shank's mare: a saying referring to walking somewhere when one should be riding a horse

lame: having a body part injured enough so as to be unable to get around without pain or difficulty

inevitable: sure to happen; certain

cinch: a band used to fasten a saddle

tack rail: a rack designed to hold a saddle, bridle, and other riding equipment

bay: red with black points

buffer: a material for reducing shock resulting from contact

rigors: difficulties; harshness

liniment: a liquid medicine rubbed on the skin especially to relieve pain

Comprehension Questions

1. What was wrong with Owen's horse, Grayson?
2. What difficult decision did Owen have to make concerning Grayson? Why was this decision such a difficult one for Owen to make?
3. What fond memory of Grayson does Owen recall as he is caring for him in the stall?
4. What decision does Owen make regarding Grayson? How does this decision make him feel?
5. Have you ever had a pet? If so, describe your relationship with him or her.

Extension Activity

Write a sequel to "The Last Ride." Include details about Grayson being retired to the north pasture, as well as details about Owen breaking in Cimarron.

If There Ever Was a Pair

Tom Sheehan

This poem echoes the important relationship between a cowboy and his horse.

Even though the cowboy's free,
his horse will chart his destiny,
for if there ever was a pair,
it's the cowboy on his **mare**,

Or a **stallion** black and bold
whose **lineage**'s not been told,
but whose heart was dealt to him
when he was born black and trim.

Man and horse, they say is true,
coupled in the prairie view,
born to be a one-way paddle
as they share a single saddle.

Mark the man who gives his horse
the greater share of water's course,
and mark that horse when man's aground
and needs four legs to get around.

Know such pairing gave its best
when they opened all the West,
for their legends oft inspire
writer's vision or camper's fire.

Vocabulary

mare: an adult female horse

stallion: a male horse

lineage: the ancestors from whom one is descended

The Capture of Father Time

L. Frank Baum

This fairy tale tells what happens when a boy accidentally **lassoes** *time.*

Jim was the son of a cowboy and lived on the broad plains of Arizona. His father had trained him to lasso a bronco or a young bull with perfect accuracy, and, had Jim possessed the strength to back up his skill, he would have been as good a cowboy as any in all Arizona.

When he was twelve years old, he made his first visit to the East, where Uncle Charles, his father's brother, lived. Of course, Jim took his lasso with him, for he was proud of his skill in casting it and wanted to show his cousins what a cowboy could do.

At first the city boys and girls were much interested in watching Jim lasso posts and fence pickets, but they soon tired of it, and even Jim decided it was not the right sort of sport for cities.

But one day the butcher asked Jim to ride one of his horses into the country to a pasture, and Jim eagerly consented. He had been longing for a horseback ride, and to make it seem like old times he took his lasso with him.

He rode through the streets **demurely** enough, but on reaching the open country roads his spirits broke forth into wild **jubilation**, and, urging the butcher's horse to full gallop, he dashed away in true cowboy fashion.

Then he wanted still more liberty, and, letting down the bars that led into a big field, he began riding over the meadow and throwing his lasso at imaginary cattle, while he yelled and whooped to his heart's content.

Suddenly, on making a long cast with his lasso, the loop caught upon something and rested about three feet from the ground, while the rope drew **taut** and nearly pulled Jim from his horse.

This was unexpected. More than that, it was wonderful; for the field seemed bare of even a stump. Jim's eyes grew big with amazement, but he knew he had caught something when a voice cried out, "Here, let go! Let go, I say! Can't you see what you've done?"

No, Jim couldn't see, nor did he intend to let go until he found out what was holding the loop of the lasso. So he resorted to an old trick his father had taught him and, putting the butcher's horse to a run, began riding in a circle around the spot where his lasso had caught.

As he thus drew nearer and nearer his **quarry,** he saw the rope coil up, yet it looked to be coiling over nothing but air. One end of the lasso was made fast to a ring in the saddle, and when the rope was almost wound up and the horse began to pull away and snort with fear, Jim **dismounted**. Holding the reins of the bridle in one hand, he followed the rope, and an instant later saw an old man caught fast in the coils of the lasso.

His head was bald and uncovered, but long white whiskers grew down to his waist. About his body was thrown a loose robe of fine white linen. In one hand he bore a great **scythe**, and beneath the other arm he carried an hourglass.

While Jim gazed wonderingly upon him, this **venerable** old man spoke in an angry voice, "Now, then—get that rope off as fast as you can! You've brought everything on earth to a standstill by your foolishness! Well—what are you staring at? Don't you know who I am?"

"No," said Jim stupidly.

"Well, I'm Time—Father Time! Now, make haste and set me free—if you want the world to run properly."

"How did I happen to catch you?" asked Jim, without making a move to release his captive.

"I don't know. I've never been caught before," growled Father Time. "But I suppose it was because you were foolishly throwing your lasso at nothing."

"I didn't see you," said Jim.

"Of course, you didn't. I'm invisible to the eyes of human beings unless they get within three feet of me, and I take care to keep more than that distance away from them. That's why I was crossing this field, where I supposed no one would be. And

I should have been perfectly safe had it not been for your beastly lasso. Now, then," he added crossly, "are you going to get that rope off?"

"Why should I?" asked Jim.

"Because everything in the world stopped moving the moment you caught me. I don't suppose you want to make an end of all business and pleasure, and war and love, and misery and ambition and everything else, do you? Not a watch has ticked since you tied me up here like a mummy!"

Jim laughed. It really was funny to see the old man wound round and round with coils of rope from his knees up to his chin.

"It'll do you good to rest," said the boy. "From all I've heard, you lead a rather busy life."

"Indeed, I do," replied Father Time, with a sigh. "I'm due in **Kamchatka** this very minute. And to think one small boy is upsetting all my regular habits!"

"Too bad!" said Jim, with a grin. "But since the world has stopped anyhow, it won't matter if it takes a little longer recess. As soon as I let you go Time will fly again. Where are your wings?"

"I haven't any," answered the old man. "That is a story cooked up by someone who never saw me. As a matter of fact, I move rather slowly."

"I see, you take your time," remarked the boy. "What do you use that scythe for?"

"To mow down the people," said the ancient one. "Every time I swing my scythe someone dies."

"Then I ought to win a life-saving medal by keeping you tied up," said Jim. "Some folks will live this much longer."

"But they won't know it," said Father Time, with a sad smile; "so it will do them no good. You may as well untie me at once."

"No," said Jim, with a determined air. "I may never capture you again; so I'll hold you for a while and see how the world wags without you."

Then he swung the old man, bound as he was, upon the back of the butcher's horse, and, getting into the saddle himself, started back toward town, one hand holding his prisoner and the other guiding the reins.

When he reached the road, his eye fell on a strange **tableau**. A horse and buggy stood in the middle of the road, the horse in the act of trotting, with his head held high and two legs in the air, but perfectly motionless. In the buggy a man and a woman were seated; but had they been turned into stone they could not have been more still and stiff.

"There's no Time for them!" sighed the old man. "Won't you let me go now?"

"Not yet," replied the boy.

He rode on until he reached the city, where all the people stood in exactly the same positions they were in when Jim lassoed Father Time. Stopping in front of a big dry goods store, the boy hitched his horse and went in. The clerks were measuring out goods and showing patterns to the rows of customers in front of them, but everyone seemed suddenly to have become a statue.

There was something very unpleasant in this scene, and a cold shiver began to run up and down Jim's back; so he hurried out again.

On the edge of the sidewalk sat a poor, crippled beggar, holding out his hat, and beside him stood a prosperous-looking gentleman who was about to drop a penny into the beggar's hat. Jim knew this gentleman to be very rich but rather stingy, so he ventured to run his hand into the man's pocket and take out his purse, in which was a $20 gold piece. This glittering coin he put in the gentleman's fingers instead of the penny and then restored the purse to the rich man's pocket.

"That donation will surprise him when he comes to life," thought the boy.

He mounted the horse again and rode up the street. As he passed the shop of his friend, the butcher, he noticed several pieces of meat hanging outside.

"I'm afraid that meat will spoil," he remarked.

"It takes Time to spoil meat," answered the old man.

This struck Jim as being queer, but true.

"It seems Time meddles with everything," said he.

"Yes; you've made a prisoner of the most important **personage** in the world," groaned the old man, "and you haven't enough sense to let him go again."

Jim did not reply, and soon they came to his uncle's house, where he again dismounted. The street was filled with teams and people, but all were motionless. His two little cousins were just coming out the gate on their way to school, with their books and **slates** underneath their arms; so Jim had to jump over the fence to avoid knocking them down.

In the front room sat his aunt, reading her Bible. She was just turning a page when Time stopped. In the dining room was his uncle, finishing his luncheon. His mouth was open and his fork **poised** just before it, while his eyes were fixed upon the newspaper folded beside him.

Jim helped himself to his uncle's pie, and while he ate it he walked out to his prisoner.

"There's one thing I don't understand," said he.

"What's that?" asked Father Time.

"Why is it that I'm able to move around while everyone else is—is—froze up?"

"That is because I'm your prisoner," answered the other. "You can do anything you wish with Time now. But unless you are careful, you'll do something you will be sorry for."

Jim threw the crust of his pie at a bird that was suspended in the air, where it had been flying when Time stopped.

"Anyway," he laughed, "I'm living longer than anyone else. No one will ever be able to catch up with me again."

"Each life has its allotted span," said the old man. "When you have lived your proper time, my scythe will mow you down."

"I forgot your scythe," said Jim thoughtfully.

Then a spirit of mischief came into the boy's head, for he happened to think that the present opportunity to have fun would never occur again. He tied Father Time to his uncle's hitching post, that he might not escape, and then crossed the road to the corner grocery.

The grocer had scolded Jim that very morning for stepping into a basket of turnips by accident. So the boy went to the back end of the grocery and turned on the faucet of the molasses barrel.

"That'll make a nice mess when Time starts the molasses running all over the floor," said Jim, with a laugh.

A little further down the street was a barber shop, and sitting in the barber's chair Jim saw the man that all the boys declared was the "meanest man in town." He certainly did not like the boys, and the boys knew it. The barber was in the act of shampooing this person when Time was captured. Jim ran to the drug store, and, getting a bottle of **mucilage**, he returned and poured it over the ruffled hair of the unpopular citizen.

"That'll probably surprise him when he wakes up," thought Jim.

Nearby was the schoolhouse. Jim entered it and found that only a few of the pupils were assembled. But the teacher sat at his desk, stern and frowning as usual.

Taking a piece of chalk, Jim marked upon the blackboard in big letters the following words:

"Every scholar is requested to yell the minute he enters the room. He will also please throw his books at the teacher's head. Signed, Prof. Sharpe."

"That ought to raise a nice **rumpus**," murmured the mischief-maker, as he walked away.

On the corner stood Policeman Mulligan, talking with old Miss Scrapple, the worst gossip in town, who always delighted in saying something disagreeable about her neighbors. Jim thought this opportunity was too good to lose. So he took off the policeman's cap and brass-buttoned coat and put them on Miss Scrapple, while the lady's feathered and ribboned hat he placed **jauntily** upon the policeman's head.

The effect was so comical that the boy laughed aloud, and as a good many people were standing near the corner Jim decided that Miss Scrapple and Officer Mulligan would create a sensation when Time started upon his travels.

Then the young cowboy remembered his prisoner, and, walking back to the hitching post, he came within three feet of it and saw Father Time still standing patiently within the coils of the lasso. He looked angry and annoyed, however, and growled out, "Well, when do you intend to release me?"

"I've been thinking about that ugly scythe of yours," said Jim.

"What about it?" asked Father Time.

"Perhaps if I let you go you'll swing it at me the first thing, to be revenged," replied the boy.

Father Time gave him a severe look, but said, "I've known boys for thousands of years, and, of course, I know they're mischievous and reckless. But I like boys because they grow up to be men and populate my world. Now, if a man had caught me by accident, as you did, I could have scared him into letting me go instantly; but boys are harder to scare. I don't know as I blame you. I was a boy myself, long ago, when the world was new. But surely you've had enough fun with me by this time, and now I hope you'll show the respect that is due to old age. Let me go, and in return I will promise to forget all about my capture. The incident won't do much harm, anyway, for no one will ever know that Time has halted the last three hours or so."

"All right," said Jim cheerfully, "since you've promised not to mow me down, I'll let you go." But he had a notion some people in the town would suspect Time had stopped when they returned to life.

He carefully unwound the rope from the old man, who, when he was free, at once shouldered his scythe, rearranged his white robe, and nodded farewell.

The next moment he had disappeared, and with a rustle and rumble and roar of activity the world came to life again and jogged along as it always had before.

Jim wound up his lasso, mounted the butcher's horse, and rode slowly down the street.

Loud screams came from the corner, where a great crowd of people quickly assembled. From his seat on the horse, Jim saw Miss Scrapple, attired in the policeman's uniform, angrily shaking her fists in Mulligan's face, while the officer was furiously stamping upon the lady's hat, which he had torn from his own head amidst the **jeers** of the crowd.

As he rode past the schoolhouse, he heard a tremendous chorus of yells and knew Prof. Sharpe was having a hard time **quelling** the riot caused by the sign on the blackboard.

Through the window of the barber shop, he saw the "mean man" frantically **belaboring** the barber with a hair brush, while his hair stood up stiff as **bayonets** in all directions. And the grocer ran out of his door and yelled "Fire!" while his shoes left a track of molasses wherever he stepped.

Jim's heart was filled with joy. He was fairly reveling in the excitement he had caused when someone caught his leg and pulled him from the horse.

"What're ye doin' hear, ye rascal?" cried the butcher angrily; "didn't ye promise to put that beast inter Plympton's pasture? An' now I find ye ridin' the poor nag around like a gentleman o' leisure!"

"That's a fact," said Jim, with surprise; "I clean forgot about the horse!"

Vocabulary

lasso: to catch livestock with a rope

demurely: in a reserved manner

jubilation: joy

taut: drawn tightly

quarry: something chased after

dismounted: to get down from a horse

scythe: a tool that has a curved blade on a long curved handle and is used for mowing grass or grain by hand

venerable: impressive because of age

Kamchatka: a peninsula 750 miles (1207 kilometers) long in Eastern Russia

tableau: a scene shown by a group of people who remain silent and motionless

personage: an important or famous person

slates: tablets of material, such as slate, used for writing on

poised: held in a steady position

mucilage: a glue-like substance

rumpus: a state of noisy, confused activity; commotion

jauntily: in a quick and spirited manner

jeers: negative comments

quell: to put a stop to

belaboring: attacking with blows

bayonets: weapons like daggers made to fit on the end of a rifle

Comprehension Questions

1. Why didn't Jim see Father Time when he lassoed him?
2. Why wouldn't Jim let Father Time go?
3. Name at least two mischievous things Jim did during the time when Father Time was captured.
4. Father Time told Jim, "Each life has its allotted span. When you have lived your proper time, my scythe will mow you down." While we know Father Time is not real, do you think there is some truth to the statement that each life has a predetermined length?

Extension Activity

Many fairy tales have common elements. Fill out the Fairy Tale Analysis sheet on page 15 of the Student Exercises *booklet to further analyze "The Capture of Father Time."*

Unit 8
Tales of the Rails

John Henry: A Steel Driving Wonder

Traditional tale, adapted by Elizabeth Kearney

While there are disputes as to whether John Henry truly existed, legend has it that John Henry was born a slave, but began his work for the railroad after the Civil War. At that time, railroads had begun to link the states together. Folks would travel from one side of the country to the other in less than a week, when they had been used to it taking months! The railroad companies had thousands of employees working to create the smooth, flat pathways required by trains. John Henry was the most renowned worker of them all.

Let's see… Where should I begin? Well, he was strong—that's for sure. No, maybe strong is too simple a word. He was muscular and mighty and full of firepower. And that's just the beginning.

On the night when John Henry was born, it was dark and stormy, and lightning filled the sky. His proud parents probably should have taken that as a sign that John was not your normal baby. But not to worry—they soon realized this when he grew as fast as a summer cornstalk.

It was when he was a teenager that he heard the call of the railroad.

He picked up a hammer and said to his mama, "A hammer will be the death of me." He longed to be a steel driver. Steel drivers helped make the pathways for the railroad lines by cutting holes in the rock with steel drills or spikes. Then they placed dynamite in the holes. Well, it didn't take long before John Henry's size and strength got him a fine reputation and an offer from the wealthy Chesapeake and Ohio Railroad, also known as the C&O.

They knew his wife Pollie Ann was the best cook that side of the Mississippi, so they offered her a job, too, as head cook of the whole outfit. So, off John Henry and Pollie Ann went to work on the railroad **extension** line from the Chesapeake Bay to the Ohio Valley.

These C&O folks hoped that John Henry would help them with a little problem they had. They had to figure a way to build their railroad around a huge mountain called Big Bend in West

Virginia. John Henry spoke up and told those **bigwigs** there was no problem at all. They could build a tunnel right *through* that mountain.

Soon he was known as "King of Steel Drivers." His hammer moved as fast as that lightning that lit up the sky the night he was born. That summer was hotter than live coal, and many of the men took to taking long breaks while John Henry kept drivin' that steel.

When the men thanked him, he just smiled that big smile of his and said, "A man ain't nothing but a man. He has just got to do his best." When he was done digging each day, John Henry would pull out his banjo. He would play and sing with a sweet, deep voice, and the railroad workers sure did appreciate it.

One day that September, a slick-looking salesman named Mr. Stephens came to town. He told the head of the C&O Railroad that he was selling a tool that would save him time and money. It was a steam-powered drill that could do the work of more than a dozen men. Now, the captain liked the idea of saving money, but he had more confidence in John Henry than he did a smooth salesman.

So he yelled to John Henry, "This here man says his fancy new drill can outwork even you."

Well, John Henry was a patient man, but he didn't like the attitude of this city slicker. He took that as a challenge, and what happened next would go down in history as the most famous contest between man and machine.

At 8:00 the following morning, a ring of the dinner bell marked the beginning of a race. Mr. Stephens was armed with his fancy steam-powered drill, and John had his trusty hammer. They would go as far as they could through that mountain by 3:00 p.m. A large, curious crowd soon gathered around. John Henry gave his hammer a little kiss, and away he went.

At first, Mr. Stephens had some trouble. You see, he needed to wear protective gear to run that steam-powered drill. By the time he got his special outfit on, John Henry was already driving his second steel rod into the mountain. At 12:00, the lunch bell rang and the race **ceased** for a while. John Henry laughed and joked with his friends while he ate Pollie's fine cooking. Then he gave her a kiss, and back to work he went.

An afternoon shower soon began, but this didn't bother John Henry. However, the fancy steam-powered drill required the use of a **tripod**, and it slipped around on that mountain **terrain** like a fish out of water. Meanwhile, John Henry started on his third rod. Soon, though, the sun came out strong and fierce. John Henry started to sweat **profusely**, and the captain warned him against heat exhaustion. John Henry's coworkers took turns throwing buckets of water on him to cool him off, but the heat seemed to be taking its toll. Soon, they noticed he was missing the steel rod with his hammer more often than he was hitting it. Pollie pleaded with John Henry to stop, but he just kept on.

At 3:00 the finish bell rang. Mr. Stephens stopped the steam-powered drill, and John fell to his knees. The captain and one of Mr. Stephens's friends ran over to do the measuring. They agreed that the steam-powered drill had gone ten feet, and John Henry had hand driven solid steel rods fourteen feet into the mountain. Man had prevailed over machine.

Out of the sound of the cheering crowd came John Henry's scream, "I beat it! I did it!" and then he collapsed. The captain and his men ran to him, picked up his heavy body, and loaded him onto a wagon in order to take him back to his tent. Before the wagon could get started, John Henry breathed his last breath. Pollie was at his side holding his hand.

John Henry died September 30, 1887. The doctor said it could have been his heart, or it could have simply been that the heat took its toll on poor John's body. He was buried by the very mountain that made him so famous. Pollie stayed on as cook with the railroad until the line from the Chesapeake Bay to the Ohio Valley was finished. Then the railroad company bought her a little house near John Henry's grave.

Years later, the steam drill did replace the steel drivers. The steel drivers took other jobs, but no matter their profession, they told stories and sang songs of their hero, John Henry.

Vocabulary

extension: the state of being made longer

bigwigs: people who are important or think they are important

ceased: stopped

tripod: a stand that has three legs

terrain: the surface features of an area of land

profusely: pouring forth in great amounts

Comprehension Questions

1. What was John Henry's solution to the C&O's problem of having to build train tracks around Big Bend Mountain?
2. During the race between John Henry and Mr. Stephens, what problems put Mr. Stephens at a disadvantage?
3. How did the legend of John Henry live on even after he died?
4. A simile is a comparison using the words *like* or *as*. For example, "the toddler was as busy as a bee." Find at least two similes in the story.

Extension Activity

Visit the following website to learn more about John Henry:

⇨ http://www.ibiblio.org/john_henry/

John Henry, Steel Driving Man

Songs about John Henry began to be written and sung soon after his death. This song was written by W. T. Blankenship about 1900, but it represented portions of several earlier versions.

John Henry was a railroad man,
He worked from six 'till five,
"Raise 'em up bullies and let 'em drop down,
I'll beat you to the bottom or die."

John Henry said to his captain,
"You are nothing but a common man,
Before that steam drill shall beat me down,
I'll die with my hammer in my hand."

John Henry said to the **shakers**,
"You must listen to my call.
Before that steam drill shall beat me down,
I'll **jar** these mountains till they fall."

John Henry's captain said to him,
"I believe these mountains are caving in."
John Henry said to his captain, "Oh, Lord!
That's my hammer you hear in the wind."

John Henry he said to his captain,
"Your money is getting mighty slim.
When I hammer through this old mountain,
Oh, Captain, will you walk in?"

John Henry's captain came to him
With fifty dollars in his hand.
He laid his hand on his shoulder and said,
"This belongs to a steel driving man."

John Henry was hammering on the right side,
The big steam drill on the left.
Before that steam drill could beat him down,
He hammered his fool self to death.

They carried John Henry to the mountains;
From his shoulder his hammer would ring.
She caught on fire by a little blue blaze—
I believe these old mountains are caving in.

John Henry was lying on his death bed;
He turned over on his side,
And these were the last words John Henry said:
"Bring me a cool drink of water before I die."

John Henry had a little woman;
Her name was Pollie Ann.
He hugged and kissed her just before he died,
Saying, "Pollie, do the very best you can."

John Henry's woman heard he was dead.
She could not rest on her bed;
She got up at midnight, caught that No. 4 train,
"I am going where John Henry fell dead."

They carried John Henry to that new burying ground,
His wife all dressed in blue;
She laid her hand on John Henry's cold face,
"John Henry, I've been true to you."

Vocabulary

shakers: the men who held the steel spikes that the hammer men pounded

jar: to cause to shake or vibrate

Thomas Hovenden

James Baldwin

Artist Thomas Hovenden is an example of a true hero.

Perhaps somewhere you have seen the painting, or if not the painting an **engraved** copy of it, entitled *A Breton Interior of 1793*. It is the picture of a humble room in a humble cottage in northern France in the time of the French Revolution. The family within are all busily occupied, preparing for defense against some unseen foe. Some are molding bullets, some are sharpening old swords, and some are **furbishing** other neglected weapons of war. It is a strong picture, **eloquent** with expression, and you will wish to study it long. Look at the engraved copy closely, and perhaps you can make out the artist's name in the corner—Thomas Hovenden.

There are other famous pictures, also, that were painted by Hovenden. One bears the name of **Tennyson's** lovely heroine, *Elaine*, and one is called *The Two Lilies*. But perhaps the most beautiful and touching of all is the picture entitled, *Breaking the Home Ties*. This painting was much admired at the World's Columbian Exposition in 1893, and it has often been copied.

Hovenden was an American artist, although his birthplace was in Ireland. He had studied under the best masters, both in America and in Paris. After years of effort and of faithful endeavor, fame and fortune seemed to be within his grasp; a life's ambition was almost realized.

One afternoon in August 1895, he left his country home near Norristown, intending to ride by trolley to the railroad sta-

tion where he would take the evening train for Philadelphia. At the outskirts of the town the passengers were required to **alight** from the first trolley car, cross the railroad tracks, and take another car on the opposite side.

Thomas Hovenden was one of the last to step out of the trolley car, and as he did so he heard the roar of a fast freight train coming with great speed down the tracks in front of him. At the same time, to his great horror, he saw a little girl, who had been on the trolley, run forward to cross the railroad. The child had not noticed the approaching train, and was intent only upon reaching the second trolley car on the farther side of the tracks.

The engineer whistled. The child looked up and saw the great engine bearing down upon her. She was paralyzed with fear. She stood motionless between the tracks.

Then it was that Thomas Hovenden, fifty-five years of age, did the heroic deed of his life. Quicker than thought, he leaped forward and seized the child. Another second for another leap, and both of them would have been in safety. But, alas, the monster engine was too quick for him. It struck him as he was almost across. Artist and child were hurled far to the side of the road. They lay there in the dust, side by side, and quite motionless.

Gentle hands hastened to lift them up. But Thomas Hovenden, artist, hero, was dead. The child for whom he had given his life was **unconscious**. They lifted her from the ground; they carried her lovingly to a neighboring house; but before the sun went down that day, she too, had ceased to breathe. Shall we believe that Thomas Hovenden's golden deed was a failure? Far nobler is it to die in the attempt to save another's life than to live as a selfish coward afraid to perform one's duty to humanity. This last act of Thomas Hovenden proved him to be a hero of the noblest type; it crowned with the highest honor his already successful life.

Vocabulary

engraved: printed from a block or plate

furbishing: cleaning; polishing

eloquent: showing feeling or meaning

Tennyson: a famous English poet

alight: get down from

unconscious: not mentally alert

Comprehension Questions

1. Explain Thomas Hovenden's heroic act.
2. How old was Hovenden when he died?
3. The story says, "Far nobler is it to die in the attempt to save another's life than to live as a selfish coward afraid

to perform one's duty to humanity." Explain what this means in relationship to this story.

Extension Activity

Visit the New York Times *website (www.nytimes.com). Search for Thomas Hovenden to read some of the articles from the 1800s about his life, death, and funeral.*

The Ballad of Casey Jones

Wallace Saunders

In the late 1800s, Casey Jones was a railroad engineer for the Illinois Central Railroad (IC). He was known for his trains being punctual, a quality well respected in an era in which railroad transportation was flourishing. On April 30, 1900, Casey took his last ride. His train crashed through the caboose of another train parked on the same track. Casey was mortally wounded by a bolt or piece of splintered lumber which struck him in the throat. Soon, songs began to be written and sung about Casey. This is one by a man named Wallace Saunders.

Come all you **rounders** if you want to hear
A story 'bout a brave engineer.
Casey Jones was the rounder's name,
'Twas on the Illinois Central that he won his fame.

Casey Jones, he loved a locomotive.
Casey Jones, a mighty man was he.
Casey Jones run his final locomotive
With the Cannonball Special on the old **I.C.**

Casey pulled into Memphis on Number Four.
The engine **foreman** met him at the **roundhouse** door;
Said, "Joe Lewis won't be able to make his run
So you'll have to double out on Number One."

If I can have Sim Webb, my fireman, my engine 382,
Although I'm tired and weary, I'll take her through.
Put on my whistle that come in today
'Cause I mean to keep her wailing as we ride and pray.

Casey Jones mounted the **cabin**,
Casey Jones, with the orders in his hand.
Casey Jones, he mounted the cabin,
Started on his farewell journey to the promised land.

They pulled out of Memphis nearly two hours late;
Soon they were speeding at a terrible rate.
And the people knew by the whistle's moan
That the man at the **throttle** was Casey Jones.

Need more coal there, fireman Sim,
Open that door and heave it in.
Give that shovel all you got
And we'll reach Canton on the dot.

On April 30, 1900, that rainy morn,
Down in Mississippi near the town of Vaughan,
Sped the Cannonball Special only two minutes late
Traveling 70 miles an hour when they saw a freight.

The caboose number 83 was on the main line;
Casey's last words were "Jump, Sim, while you have the time."
At 3:52 that morning came the fateful end;
Casey took his farewell trip to the promised land.

Casey Jones, he died at the throttle,
With the whistle in his hand.
Casey Jones, he died at the throttle,
But we'll all see Casey in the promised land.

His wife and three children were left to mourn
The tragic death of Casey on that April morn.
May God through His goodness keep them by His grace
Till they all meet together in that heavenly place.

Casey's body lies buried in Jackson, Tennessee,
Close beside the tracks of the old I.C.
May his spirit live forever throughout the land
As the greatest of all heroes of a railroad man.

Casey Jones, he died at the throttle,
Casey Jones, with the whistle in his hand.
Casey Jones, he died at the throttle,
But we'll all see Casey in the promised land.

Vocabulary

rounders: those who run or have charge of a train engine; engineers

I.C.: Illinois Central Railroad, sometimes called the Main Line of Mid-America

foreman: a person in charge of a group of workers

roundhouse: a circular building where locomotives are kept or repaired

cabin: a compartment on a train for crew or passengers

throttle: a lever connected to a valve that controls the flow of steam to an engine

Comprehension Questions

1. According to the song, why did Casey have to make the ride that day?
2. According to the song, why was the train traveling at such a fast rate of speed?
3. What does the song imply happened to Casey?
4. Where is Casey Jones's body buried?

Extension Activity

Visit the following website to read an in depth account of Casey Jones's tragic story, see photos, and more!

⇨ http://www.watervalley.net/users/caseyjones/casey.htm

Unit 9
The Twentieth Century

The Sinking of the *Lusitania*

Lawton B. Evans

Chances are, you have heard of the Titanic, *but have you heard of the* Lusitania? *Its story is equally as interesting, and as tragic.*

During World War I, it was the declared policy of Germany to **torpedo** any vessel flying an enemy flag in the waters **adjacent** to the British Isles, regardless of its character, or who was on board.

One bright morning, the first day of May 1915, the huge British liner, *Lusitania*, lay at her dock ready to sail from New York to Liverpool. Her decks were crowded with passengers. They had read in the morning papers that "vessels flying the flag of Great Britain, or any of her Allies, are liable to destruction—and that travelers sailing in the war zone on ships of Great Britain or her Allies, do so at their own risk."

In spite of this warning, the ship was crowded with a large and happy **throng**, who were not **deterred** by any threat of destruction. She steamed down the harbor amid the waving of hands from the shore and the sound of music on her deck. There were many confident souls on board, but along with them were many who were wondering if destruction really lay in wait for the great vessel.

The voyage was full of pleasure. The decks were crowded with **promenaders**, and the smoking room and cabins were centers of amusement and conversation. There was little thought of danger, and but few discussed the possibility of the ship being torpedoed. It was an event that no one wished to consider for a moment.

The morning of May 7 came with a heavy fog over the sea. The blowing of the siren awakened the passengers, and some of them commented on the fact, saying it might attract the submarines. Later on the fog lifted, leaving the sky without a cloud and the sea as smooth as glass. The shores of Ireland were in sight. Everybody was glad that the voyage was nearly over and that, in a few hours, the ship and its passengers would be safe.

The morning passed, and the ship steamed steadily on. Luncheon hour came, and the passengers thronged below for their midday meal. Nearer and nearer came the friendly shores, and less and less grew the danger that threatened the vessel. The British flag was flying, as if in defiance to the threat of Germany.

Having finished luncheon, some of the passengers came on deck, some went to their rooms to rest, while others turned to the smoking rooms. The ship settled down to the usual afternoon routine.

At a few minutes after two o'clock, some of the passengers saw what looked like a whale or porpoise, rising about three-quarters of a mile to **starboard**. They knew that it was a submarine, but no one dared name it. All eyes now fastened in silence and dread on the **menace** that lay so quietly and sullenly in the distance.

Then a long white line, making a train of bubbles across the water, started from the black object. It came straight for the ship. No one spoke until it was about sixty yards away. Then someone cried out, "It is a torpedo!"

There was no chance for the great ship to get out of the way. Its movement was too **ponderous** for the swiftly coming torpedo. It was plain that it could not miss its mark. It was aimed ahead of the vessel and timed to strike under the bridge. As the missile of death came nearer, it dived, and the passengers held their breath. Would it hit or would it miss?

Suddenly, there was a terrific explosion, and the **fore** part of the ship was torn into great holes. Pieces of the wreckage came through the upper deck and fell among the frightened passengers. Germany had carried out her threat and had dealt death to the great **transatlantic liner**!

There was no second torpedo; there was no need of one. The **boiler** exploded immediately, and the ship **listed** heavily to starboard. The passengers rushed to the high side of the deck—the **port** side. There was such a list to starboard that the lifeboats on the port side swung so far in that they could not be launched.

The vessel began to settle, and the lifeboats on the starboard side were launched. The first boat dropped clear of the ship and floated away with no one in it. One man jumped from the deck, swam toward the boat, and got in alone.

Everyone was frightened, but there was no panic. The cry was raised, "Women and children first!" These were placed in the lifeboats that were launched. The ship settled down on the starboard side, and also by the head. Those who could not get into the lifeboats trusted the life preservers and got ready for the plunge into the cold water. The officers of the ship acted with bravery and coolness, trying to launch the lifeboats and get the women and children into safety. The wireless telegraph **apparatus** was put out of commission shortly after the explosion, but not before a **distress** message, calling for help, was sent out and answered.

So quickly did the ship sink that it was impossible to get life preservers from the lower deck cabins. Many had to leap into the sea without them. The shock of the cold water was so **benumbing** that those who jumped in were not able to swim, and many of them soon sank out of sight.

With one great plunge, the stricken vessel, that so often had crossed the Atlantic, and that, only an hour before, was so full of life and power, sank head foremost into the sea. A great wave, rushing over her decks, cast the remaining passengers into the water.

Then followed a scene of **indescribable** tragedy. Two boats, full of people, were overturned. Another was swamped as the vessel went down, and still another was dragged down by catching in the **davits**. The sea was piled with wreckage to which people were clinging. Some were struggling to swim, others were depending on life preservers, and all were battling with the waves in mad endeavor to save their lives.

Women were holding on to their husbands, while both went down. Children were floating helpless, trying to catch any object and crying **piteously** for their parents, before their little mouths were closed forever.

One by one they went down beneath the cruel waves. Thus, 1,152 were drowned. Of these, 114 were known to be American citizens. Of the 2,000 and more passengers, 952 were saved in the lifeboats and on the rafts picked up by friendly vessels that hastened to the scene of disaster.

Thus did the German submarine carry out the threat of the German government and sink a noble ship with its precious freight of human lives.

Vocabulary

torpedo: a thin, cigar-shaped, self-propelled submarine weapon

adjacent: near

throng: a large number of people gathered together

deterred: discouraged

promenaders: people who are walking or strolling for pleasure

starboard: the right side of a ship or aircraft looking forward

menace: something that represents a threat; danger

ponderous: slow due to heaviness

fore: front

transatlantic: spanning or crossing the Atlantic Ocean

liner: a ship or airplane of a regular transportation line

boiler: a tank in which water is heated or hot water is stored

listed: leaned to one side

port the left side of a ship or aircraft looking forward

apparatus: instrument; device

distress: a condition of danger or desperate need

benumbing: to make numb, especially by cold

indescribable: impossible to describe

davits: a pair of posts with curved arms having ropes and pulleys attached and used especially on ships to raise and lower small boats

piteously: in a way that moves one to pity or compassion

Comprehension Questions

1. Describe the contrast between the warning from the Germans and the mood of the passengers that first day on the *Lusitania*.
2. In two to three sentences, summarize what happened when the torpedo hit the *Lusitania*.
3. How many people died in this tragedy? How many people survived?

Extension Activity

The story does not give many details about how the Lusitania's *survivors were rescued. Use the Internet to find out information and write a paragraph about how the survivors were rescued.*

The Death of the *Lusitania*

Phoebe Amory

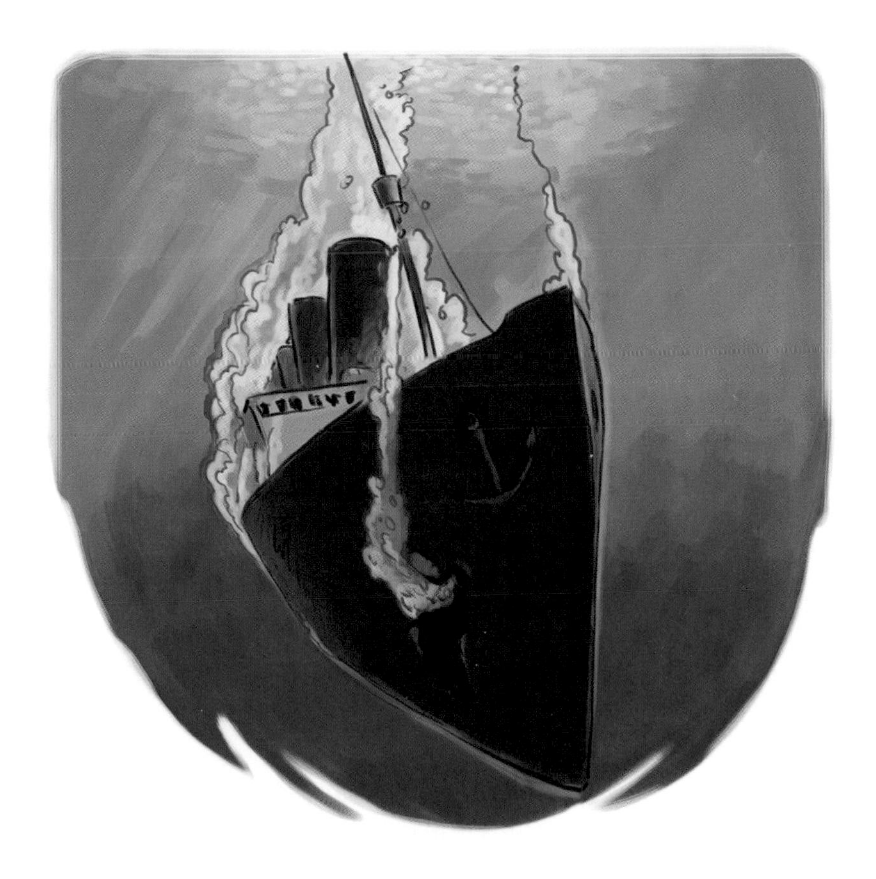

This poem was written by a Lusitania *survivor, of Toronto, Canada. In her published 1917 account, she claimed that she booked her passage in order to visit her five sons who were in military service in England.*

O *Lusitania*, **Empress** of the Sea,
Art thou dead and buried in the deep.
With all thy freight of human souls,
Victim of the **Huns**' most Hellish darts.

Come nations! Rise, **avenge** this **hideous** crime.
Avenge the cries of English hope,
now lying cold and dead in ocean deep.
Come nations! Rise and crush

This hideous **foe**: this vampire of the world,
who is no man
but just a beast of prey respecting nothing,
Laying waste to works of centuries,
Breaking hearts and homes on every side.

Come quickly, come, o'er England's blood
Be shed in vain, her **noble** sons all dead
And lying on the plains. Come, nations,
Crush this vampire into dust; come quickly, come.

O *Lusitania*, my tears are falling for thee,
Fair village of palaces, gone for evermore
Beneath the cold blue waters.

Vocabulary

empress: a woman who is ruler of an empire

Huns: a warlike central Asian people gaining control of a large part of Europe about A.D. 450; a reference to the Germans

avenge: to punish on behalf of a person for some wrong doing

hideous: horribly ugly or disgusting

foe: enemy

noble: worthy of respect

Comprehension Questions

1. How does this poem express Mrs. Amory's feelings toward the Germans after the sinking of the *Lusitania*?
2. This poem was written while World War I was still taking place. What is Mrs. Amory pleading for?

Extension Activity

Locate the article "Lest we Forget" by Jim Kalafus & Michael Poirier online to read more about Phoebe Amory and other Lusitania *survivors.*

Cher Ami

C. Douglas Sterner

How can a pigeon be a war hero? Read on to find out!

The ability to communicate is essential to soldiers in the field. Without communications to their commanders or support **units** in the rear area, soldiers on the front line can't send messages about their progress, request needed supplies, or call for help when things reach their worst.

During World War I, messages were sometimes transmitted by wire (telegraph or field phone), but two-way radio communications had not yet become available. Sometimes a unit was ordered to attack over a broad and often difficult **terrain**, making it impossible to string the wire necessary for communications. In these situations, a field commander often carried with him several carrier pigeons.

Pigeons served many purposes during the war, racing through the skies with airplanes, or even being fitted with cameras to take pictures of enemy positions. But one of the most important roles they served was as messengers. An important message would be written on a piece of paper. Next the paper would be neatly folded and secured in a small **canister** attached to a pigeon's leg. Once the pigeon was released, it would try to fly to its home back behind the lines, where the message would be read and **transmitted** to the proper military planners.

The United States Army is divided among several different specialties, the men from each specialty trained for a particular kind of work. Infantrymen are trained to fight on the ground, artillerymen are responsible for the big guns, armor refers to the men who fight in tanks, and the Air Service was the name for the group of soldiers who fought in the air during World War I. One of the oldest of these groups of soldiers is the U.S. Army Signal Corps. Since the birth of the United States, these men have been responsible for insuring that messages between all units, (including messages to other branches of service like the Navy and Marines), got through. The Army Signal Corps identifies itself by a torch with two crossed flags. These represent signal flags, a common way that messages were passed using code.

When the United States entered World War I in 1917, the Army Signal Corps was given 600 pigeons for the purpose of passing messages when it couldn't be done by signal flag or field phone. The pigeons were donated by bird breeders in Great Britain, then trained for their jobs by American soldiers.

During the Meuse-Argonne Offensive, the two-month battle that finally ended World War I, 442 pigeons were used in the area of **Verdun** to carry hundreds of messages.

This is how the system worked. When a commander in the field needed to send a message, he first wrote it out on paper, trying to be both brief and yet as detailed as possible. Then he called for one of his Signal Corps officers, who would bring one of the pigeons that went with the soldiers into battle. The message would be put in the **capsule** on the bird's leg, and then the bird would be tossed high in the air to fly home.

The carrier pigeon would fly back to his home **coop** behind the lines. When he landed, the wires in the coop would sound a bell or buzzer, and another soldier of the Signal Corps would know a message had arrived. He would go to the coop and remove the message from the canister. He would then send it by telegraph, field phone, or personal messenger to the right people.

Carrier pigeons did an important job. It was also very dangerous. If the enemy soldiers were nearby when a pigeon was released, they knew that the bird would be carrying important messages, and tried their best to shoot the pigeon down so the message couldn't be delivered.

Some of these pigeons became quite famous among the infantrymen they worked for. One pigeon, named "the Mocker," flew fifty-two missions before he was wounded. Another was named "President Wilson." He was injured in the last week of the war, and it seemed impossible for him to reach his destination. Though he lost his foot, the message got through to save a large group of surrounded American infantrymen.

Probably the most famous of all the carrier pigeons was one named Cher Ami, two French words meaning "dear friend." Cher Ami flew for several months on the front lines during the fall of 1918. He flew twelve important missions to deliver messages. Perhaps the most important was the message he carried on October 4, 1918.

Mr. Charles Whittlesey was a lawyer in New York, but when the United States called for soldiers to help France regain its freedom, Whittlesey joined the Army and went to Europe to help. He was made the commander of a **battalion** of soldiers in the 77th Infantry Division, known as the Liberty Division because most of the men came from New York and wore a bright blue patch on their shoulders that had on it the Statue of Liberty.

On October 3, 1918, Major Whittlesey and more than 500 men were trapped in a small **depression** on the side of the hill. Surrounded by enemy soldiers, many were killed and wounded in the first day. By the second day, only a little more than 200 men were still alive or unwounded.

Major Whittlesey sent out several pigeons to tell his commanders where he was and how bad the trap was. The next afternoon he had only one pigeon left, Cher Ami.

During the afternoon, the American Artillery tried to send some protection by firing hundreds of big artillery rounds into the **ravine** where the Germans surrounded Major Whittlesey and his men. Unfortunately, the American commanders didn't know exactly where the American soldiers were, and they started dropping the big shells right on top of them. It was a horrible situation that might have resulted in Major Whittlesey and all his men getting killed—by their own army!

Major Whittlesey called for his last pigeon, Cher Ami. He wrote a quick and simple note telling the men who directed the artillery guns where the Americans were located and asking them to stop. The note that was put in the canister on Cher Ami's left leg simply said:

> "We are along the road parallel to 276.4.
>
> Our own artillery is dropping a barrage directly on us.
>
> For heaven's sake, stop it."

As Cher Ami tried to fly back home, the Germans saw him rising out of the brush and opened fire. For several minutes, bullets zipped through the air all around him. For a minute it looked like the little pigeon was going to fall, that he wasn't going to make it. Cher Ami was **plummeting** to earth against a very heavy attack from German bullets.

Somehow Cher Ami managed to spread his wings and start climbing again, higher and higher beyond the range of the enemy guns. The little bird flew twenty-five miles in only twenty-five minutes to deliver his message. When he reached his coop, he could no longer fly, and the soldier that answered the sound of the bell found the little bird lying on his back, covered in blood. He had been blinded in one eye, and a bullet had hit his breastbone, making a hole the size of a quarter. From that awful hole, hanging by just a few tendons, was the almost severed leg of the brave little bird. Attached to that leg was a silver canister with the all-important message. Once again, Cher Ami wouldn't quit until he had finished his job. The shelling stopped, and more than 200 American lives were saved … all because the little bird would never quit trying.

Cher Ami became the hero of the 77th Infantry Division, and the medics worked long and hard to patch him up. When the French soldiers that the Americans were helping learned the story of Cher Ami's bravery and determination, they gave him one of their own country's great honors. Cher Ami, the brave carrier pigeon, was presented a medal called the French **Croix de guerre** with a palm leaf.

Though the dedicated medics saved Cher Ami's life, they couldn't save his leg. The men of the Division were careful to take care of the little bird that had saved 200 of their friends, and even carved a small wooden leg for him. When Cher Ami was well enough to travel, the little one-legged hero was put on a boat to the United States. The commander of all of the United States Army, the great General John J. Pershing, personally saw Cher Ami off as he departed France.

Back in the United States, the story of Cher Ami was told again and again. The little bird was in the newspapers and magazines; and it seemed that everyone knew his name. He became one of the most famous heroes of World War I. Years after the war, a man named Harry Webb Farrington decided to put together a book of poems and short stories about the men and heroes of World War I. When his book was published, it contained a special poem dedicated to Cher Ami:

Cher Ami

by Harry Webb Farrington

Cher Ami, how do you do!
Listen, let me talk to you;
I'll not hurt you, don't you see?
Come a little close to me.

Little scrawny blue and white
Messenger for men who fight,
Tell me of the deep, red scar,
There, just where no feathers are.

What about your poor lost leg?
Tell me, Cher Ami, I beg.
Boys and girls are at a loss,
How you won that Silver Cross.

"The finest fun that came to me
Was when I went with Whittlesey;
We marched so fast, so far ahead!
'We all are lost,' the keeper said;

'Mon Cher Ami—that's my dear friend—
You are the one we'll have to send;
The whole battalion now is lost,
And you must win at any cost.'

So with the message tied on tight,
I flew up straight with all my might;
Before I got up high enough,
Those watchful guns began to puff.

Machine-gun bullets came like rain,
You'd think I was an aeroplane;
And when I started to the rear, My!
The shot was coming near!

But on I flew, straight as a bee;
The wind could not catch up with me,
Until I dropped out of the air,
Into our own men's camp, so there!"

But, Cher Ami, upon my word,
You modest, modest little bird;
Now don't you know that you forgot?
Tell how your breast and leg were shot.

Cher Ami died of his multiple war wounds in 1919, less than a year after he had completed his service to the United States Army Signal Corps. Upon his death, a **taxidermist** preserved the small pigeon for future generations, a bird with a story that became an inspiration to millions over the years.

Today, visitors to the National Museum of American History, Smithsonian Institution in Washington, D.C., can still see Cher Ami, preserved for history alongside the French Croix de Guerre with palm that was awarded to him by the French government.

Vocabulary

unit: an organization within an armed force. It may consist of any number of soldiers, ships, vehicles, or aircraft.

terrain: the surface features of an area of land

canister: a small cylinder-shaped can used to hold something

transmitted: to transfer from one person or place to another

Verdun: a city in northeast France

capsule: a small compartment

coop: a cage for housing small animals

battalion: a large body of troops

depression: an area of land that is lower than the surrounding land

ravine: a small, narrow valley

plummeting: falling straight down

Croix de guerre: a medal first created in 1915 consisting of a square-cross medal on two crossed swords, hanging from a ribbon with various degree pins. The decoration was awarded during World War I and in other conflicts. It may either be bestowed as a unit award or to individuals who distinguish themselves by acts of heroism involving combat with enemy forces.

taxidermist: a person who practices taxidermy, the skill of preparing, stuffing, and mounting skins of animals

Comprehension Questions

1. Describe how a message is sent by carrier pigeon.
2. Why was a carrier pigeon's job dangerous?
3. In your own words, explain the meaning of the message Cher Ami carried.
4. Was Cher Ami's journey successful? Explain.
5. How did the French honor Cher Ami?
6. When did Cher Ami die?
7. Where can a person go to see Cher Ami's preserved body today?

Extension Activity

Read more about Cher Ami and other World War I carrier pigeons on the following websites:

- ⇨ http://b-29s-over-korea.com/Military-Award-Given-To-A-Pigeon-In-WW1/Military-Award-Given-To-A-Pigeon-In-WW1.html
- ⇨ americanhistory.si.edu/militaryhistory/collection/object.asp?ID=10
- ⇨ http://www.homeofheroes.com/wings/part1/3b_cherami.html
- ⇨ http://coleswildbird.com/2013/12/among-our-wwi-heroes-a-pigeon-named-cher-am/

The Hills Shall Not Imprison Me

Jennie Clare Adams

Miss Jennie Clare Adams became a missionary nurse at the Emmanuel Hospital in Capiz, on the island of Panay in the Philippines, in 1923. In 1941, when World War II threatened her safety, Miss Adams refused to relocate, believing that she was needed more than ever at the hospital in Capiz. On April 17, 1942, Japanese troops began operating on the island of Panay. Life became difficult for Miss Adams and the other missionaries at Emmanuel Hospital, but they kept working for the Lord. On December 20, 1943, Jennie Clare Adams and the other missionaries at Emmanuel Hospital were martyred by Japanese troops. This poem, along with many others, was found sewn into Miss Adams's pillow.

I shall not let these hills imprison me,
Where for **refuge** I've been forced to flee;
Like walls they shut me in on every side
While offering a sheltered place to hide.
Grim war that reaches out with bloody hands,
Some bitter price of every soul demands;
His cruel clutches tighten on our shores,
We felt his fingers touch our very doors
And soon the land in **smoldering** ruins lay;
Our home became an **alien** fort one day.
In wooded hills we chose to hide away
And not in concentration camp to stay.

I shall not let these hills imprison me,
Where I in **exile** weary months must be;
Their **towering** peaks conceal from hostile view,
But **screen** the sunrise and the sunset too.
The forest deep seems damp with dew and rain;
My thoughts turn homeward to a sunny plain-
The sun **emerging** from the fields of grain
And sinking into meadow land again,
For I am prairie born where wheat fields grow,
Where prairie grasses wave when breezes blow.
With eyes that yearn to gaze on distant scene,
Must I be **cloistered** in a small ravine?

I shall not let these hills imprison me;
I shall remember that I am still free.
No hills can from my soul a vision hide,
Nor hope be **shackled** long whate'er betide,
Nor faith be shaken by a troubled day,
If prairie lessons ever with me stay.
O Prairie land, whose massive **breadth** and length
Inspire the soul to greatness and to strength,
Whose sturdy trees withstand the stormy **gale**,
In spite of **droughts** their precious leaves **prevail**.
I shall be grateful then that I am free,
And say, "Those hills did not imprison me."

Vocabulary

refuge: a place that provides shelter or protection

grim: cruel; fierce

smoldering: to burn slowly and smoking

alien: relating or belonging to another country

exile: absence from one's country or home

towering: very tall

screen: separate; block

emerging: coming into view

cloistered: shut away from the world

shackled: hindered; deprived of freedom

breadth: width

gale: strong wind

droughts: long periods of weather without rain

prevail: remain

Comprehension Questions

1. Personification is a tool used by poets in which a nonliving thing is given human qualities. What is personified in the first stanza? What human qualities is it given?
2. The poet begins each stanza with the words, "I shall not let these hills imprison me". Explain what you think she means by this.
3. In the last stanza, the poet refers to prairie land and trees. How do these things serve as a sort of strength to her?

Wheels

Wayne Roe

The Vietnam War took place in Vietnam, Laos, and Cambodia from 1955 until 1975. The United States was involved from 1955 until 1973. Although this story is fictional, it will give you a true picture of what it was like to fight in the Vietnam War.

The old man turns in his bed. He has just fallen asleep. He settles down, but his breathing is heavy. His eyes start to twitch back and forth. The old man goes to the place he hates to be—his own dark dreams. The jungle is pitch black, but he can hear and smell them coming. He's on his belly hiding in the jungle leaves. There are three of them, and they make a triangle shape and slowly close in. The Vietnamese know where he is, and he knows they're coming. He waits until the last second; then he springs up from the ground. He pulls the trigger on his rifle, and there is silence.

The only thing he has for survival fails him. His rifle is jammed. The four just stand there and look into the whites of each other's eyes. The Vietnamese have **bayonets** on the ends of their rifles. They plunge at him. One stabs him in his arm, and he drops his rifle. Another one stabs him in the leg, and he falls to his knees. He moans in agony. The last one shoves the bayonet through his back and into his heart. The last word he whispers through his lips is "Jesus." He falls forward, and right before his face slams to the ground, he awakens from his nightmare.

Vietnam veteran Joel Simpson pulls himself to a sitting position in bed. His wife reaches over and caresses his arm for comfort. There's no need for words to be spoken. They have been through this before.

That morning Joel looks out the sunroom window with a cup of coffee in hand. The Kentucky fields are beautiful in the mornings. Today his grandson Chad is coming over for a visit. Chad is a senior in high school, and he's doing a report on the Vietnam War. Joel has never talked with his family about his experiences in the war. But something stirred in Joel's heart the other day when Chad called and asked if he would talk to him. Sometimes people just need to be asked. Maybe after all these years he needs to go back into his memories and tell his account of the war—Joel's own war story.

Chad walks into the room and embraces his grandfather. There is a genuine love between them. At first they talk about school and Chad's girlfriend. Then Joel smiles at his grandson and tells him to get his paper and pen out. The old man lets the walls down in his mind. He lets all the memories come back that have been haunting him for years. He is ready to face them again after all this time.

Joel starts his story and goes all the way back to his high school days. In school he was nicknamed "Wheels." Joel was a runner; he did not run like the wind—he ran with the wind. All of the colleges were after him. A talent like this is very rare. There's excitement in Joel's voice as he talks, and adventure in his eyes as he goes back in the past.

> It was the summer of '66. I was just a month out of high school and looking forward to going on to college. I wanted to attend a Baptist school and so was really hoping to get a track scholarship from Baylor University, but had not heard anything definite yet. If I didn't get a scholarship, I wouldn't have enough money to go to college.

I flew through the front door one afternoon and yelled for my mother. "What's for supper, Mom?" She called for me to come into the kitchen; my parents had been waiting for me to get home. I walked into the kitchen, and my dad was holding a letter.

"A letter came in the mail today, son. It's for you."

"A letter from Baylor?" I asked.

My father was sitting in the kitchen chair looking discouraged and drained. He looked at me as if he wished he could take this responsibility for me. But he knew wishing was a waste of time.

"Son, it's a letter from the United States government. You have been drafted into the Army." My father handed the letter to me.

The news was a blow to me, and I needed time to think. I knew this day might happen when I signed up for the **draft** a couple of months before. Since I was not in college yet, I had not been eligible for an **education deferment** from the draft. I had really hoped to go on to college, and being drafted into the Army might mean that I would be sent to Vietnam.

"I'll be up in my room, Mom and Dad." I slowly walked to the stairs looking down at the letter, leaving my parents wrapped in each other's arms quietly weeping.

I could hear my mother praying through her tears, "God, take care of him." The fighting in Vietnam was heating up, and they were afraid I might be sent there.

I lay on my bed and read the letter over and over. My heart felt as if it was pounding out of my chest. Fear of the unknown was upon me. I felt like I was going to throw up. I breathed in and out slowly, and asked God to give me some kind of comfort. I reached for the Bible on my nightstand and looked at the black cover. I grew up in church and believed in God and His Son Jesus. But now I felt alone and afraid. Lying there, I promised God I would take my Bible with me for strength and guidance. I rolled out of bed and put on my running shoes. I hit the sidewalk and ran myself to exhaustion.

A few days later, I was on a bus to **basic training**. The bus rolled to a stop in front of a big iron gate. The sign read "Fort

Bliss." The gate opened, and the bus drove to the basic training area and stopped at the main **compound**. All the new **recruits** got out and made a single file line. I was last to get off and get in line. I noticed how different the area around Fort Bliss looked than where I came from. It was a lot drier than it was near San Antonio.

We recruits all came from different Texas towns and had different **ethnic** backgrounds. In a short time, however, we would have one thing in common: we would all be torn down and built back up to be soldiers. We would soon learn how to do things "the army way." We would learn how to fight for each other and our country. Some would cry together, some would pray together, and some would die together.

We all settled in and got our shots and army haircuts. Next, we were given our green **fatigues** and shown to our bunks. Big Jim Ellis bunked to the right of me, and Ed Morales was to the left. Jim was the biggest guy I had ever met. A very quiet guy, Jim always kept to himself. The days of hard running and physical discipline were upon us. But I loved the running, and they started calling me "Speed."

Finally I said, "Back home they call me Wheels." So Wheels became my nickname in Nam, as well.

At night when we had a little time to ourselves, I would read God's Word. After a couple of weeks of everyone getting to know each other, some guys came over and we started having a study at night. Big Jim and Ed never joined in, but I knew they were listening. One night Mike Barnett and a few of the other guys came over to the study for a visit. Barnett did all the talking.

"You Jesus freaks make me sick to my stomach!"

The statement threw me back. I was not here to fight with Barnett and his buddies. I said what came to my heart and not my mind. I said it with a smile.

"You're always welcome to join us, Mike."

Big Jim Ellis laid down the letter he had read for the sixth time, stood up, walked over to Barnett, and looked down at him. With a monotone but very stern voice, Jim spoke. He was inches from Barnett's face.

"They have the choice to read God's Word. You have the choice not to. There's nothing else to say about this."

Barnett looked into the eyes of Big Jim for a couple of seconds, and then turned and walked away.

Ed Morales didn't even look up from the letter he was writing when he said, "We are going to need God on our side where we are probably going."

Six weeks later, our basic training was done. It was then time to begin our military specialty training. Many of us, including Big Jim, Ed, and myself were sent elsewhere to **infantry school**. There we were taught **essential combat** skills. After a month, we finished and received our orders. I had hoped I might get assigned to Fort Hood, which is not far from home, or maybe Germany. However, the Army felt it needed me, as well Big Jim and Ed, in Vietnam. My parents' worst fears had come true. At least the three of us were going to be together.

I received four weeks leave and went home to spend them with my parents. I was able to spend Christmas with them; however, it was soon time to go. Leaving home was one of the hardest things I have ever done. My mother wept, and the tears ran down my face as well. My father shook my hand and gave me a hug. He told me to trust in God. My father had no tears that day. But I found out later in a letter from my mother that he went into their bedroom and fell apart when I left. I realized he was standing tall for me. Dad knew something about war, having fought in the Philippines in 1944 and 1945.

Right after New Year's Day, 1967, I flew from San Antonio to Seattle and then went to Fort Lewis to wait for the flight to Vietnam. There I met up with Ed and Jim. Before we knew it, we were flying to Pleiku, a city in the Central Highlands. The pilot dipped the nose of the plane down. We were getting ready to land in Vietnam. You could feel the heat change as we got closer to land. The doors opened, and we stepped out and got in line. It felt like the dead of summer, and the heat was unbearable at first. The heat hits you like a sledgehammer to the stomach. It tries to suck the air from your lungs. The Texas heat was calm compared to this. Plus this place had its own smell. My mind told me it was the smell of death, but I would find out soon enough what that was like.

The base camp was stationed in a wide-open field. You could see the jungle in the distance. The camp was chaos. Men were running in every direction, and choppers were flying in and landing with the wounded and the dead. Then it finally hit home that I was really at war. My knees turned weak, and the fear made my muscles tense and brought on the shakes. I needed to move; I needed to run. Just standing there was driving me nuts inside, but we had to stay together waiting on Staff Sergeant Dunn. He returned with our orders. We had been assigned to the "Wolfhounds" **battalion** of the 25th Infantry Division. Sergeant Dunn would be our new **platoon sergeant**.

We first would spend a few days taking classes learning about Vietnam. Then we would be taken by truck to our unit's base camp in the country. Two days after getting to our base camp, we would take a couple of Huey helicopters—what we called "Slicks"—out on our first combat patrol and be dropped out in the bush of the Central Highlands. Our mission would be to head north after we landed. Our job was to seek and destroy.

Before going on about my first mission, let me tell you a little about where I was stationed. The Highlands were an area of hills and **plateaus** usually covered by jungle. Temperatures during the day would usually be between 100 and 115 degrees but would drop to around 80 at night. Night could actually feel pretty cold after the high daytime temperatures. We would often go out on patrol up and down the hills for several days at a time, carrying 60–80 pounds of equipment in our **ruck sacks**.

There wasn't much talking as we flew over the jungle heading to our destination. The sounds of the helicopter blades put you almost in a trance. We fought against the fear inside of us—the fear that death might be waiting for us. I bowed my head and prayed for protection and guidance—and for all the other men that were around me.

Sergeant Dunn broke the silence. "Don't be fooled by the beauty of this place. There is no beauty in war. Trust no one, not even women or children. Only trust your own. We fight as a unit, and we watch each other's backs at all times. And no one is left behind."

We descended down toward an open field next to the jungle and land. We got ready to jump out of the Hueys.

"Move it! Move it! Let's go—move it!

The helicopters **hovered** just above the ground, and we were to jump down to the ground. After the jump, we were to spread out in the tall grass. With all the heavy gear, we hoped we didn't land on something.

The nineteen of us all made the jump and grouped together. It was getting dark, and we needed to get away from this spot. We started making our way through the jungle. Every nerve and every sense I had were used to the max. I tried to adjust to my new surroundings. The jungle was all around me—top, bottom, and sides. The sounds made my skin crawl. I tried to keep my eyes on everything and everyone at once, but it turned into a useless attempt. I had to look for booby traps and **land mines**. I knew they were there, just like the enemy was, waiting for us.

We made camp that night, and nothing happened. I thanked the Lord in my prayers and asked for peace. My insides were a wreck. I even fought the enemy called "fear." The days went by, and we saw no enemies. But I knew war would come out of nowhere and be thrown in our faces. By then, the jungle was also our enemy. The heat and mosquitoes were just the beginning of the hell over there. My feet often got wet when crossing small creeks and rivers. I worried about foot rot, and got used to burning the leeches off my body.

For five days we fought against the jungle, and fatigue was setting in. We heard the sounds of shooting in the distance. I tried to keep my mind focused, but it slipped to better times in my life. I thought of my mother and father, and my hopes of attending college. Then, when I least expected it, they attacked. I heard the sound—crack, crack, crack—and I dove to the ground. I looked around, and all I heard was a humming noise in my head. I was in total shock. Big Jim Ellis was about six feet to the right, shooting straight ahead. I turned, got up on one knee, and just started unloading my gun into the jungle. The firefight went on for five to six minutes, tops.

Then there was only silence. But the sound of war still echoed in my ears. We stayed down for the longest time, waiting for another attack. We unloaded again, but there was no backfire. We slowly worked our way to their position—no bodies anywhere, just body parts and blood all over the place. How many did we kill? Did I kill any? God, help me. Two were wounded and four were dead from our group. I looked upon the dead and prayed for their families. Then everything in me came up, and I spit it out to the jungle.

Joel then reads a letter to Chad he had written to his folks six months after being stationed in Vietnam. It gives a pretty good idea of what he was feeling at the time.

Dear Mom and Dad,

Six months I have been over here now. But it feels like I have been here forever. I am sorry the letters are getting farther and farther apart. We are moving deeper and deeper into the war zones. I have killed many of the enemy now. I am sorry to write that, but I have to tell someone. I cannot keep it inside. I am not proud that I am killing, but I fight for my country. And that at times is not enough to keep me going. I must rely on God and His Son Jesus. But does God still love me when I am killing? Or does He turn His back on me? Pray for me, your son, that my faith stays strong in God and His ways. But there is a light of hope over here. Some men have asked to hear God's Word when we have time to sit or take breaks at night. It helps me to keep my mind on Jesus. I miss your cooking, Mom, and I miss reading God's Word with you, Dad. And pray for the family of Big Jim Ellis. Two days ago he was killed in cross fire. The bullet went through the side of his head. He died instantly. We were fighting side by side. He was my friend. Death is all around me, but I will not accept it. I cannot let death **callous** *my heart and keep me from God. I know God is for me and not against me. But in times of weakness I question if He is even here. At times it feels like death is the only one here.*

I am sorry this letter sounds so down. I am doing the best I can. I am just trying to find my way. I love and miss you both.

Your son,

Joel

It felt like the gunfire would never stop. We had been buried down for three hours fighting the **Vietcong**. Then the silence came again. You could hear the wounded and the dying calling out for help. Some of the dying asked God to help them. Some cursed God, and some cried out to their loved ones. Some just wept.

I lay there on the jungle ground wondering when my turn would come. Would I be half blown away fighting to stay alive till my last breath? Or would I die like Big Jim Ellis? The silence was broken when Sergeant Dunn yelled my name.

"Wheels, there's a man down on the left flank about thirty yards deep. Get him back here now!"

One of my duties for my battalion was to get the wounded or dead back to our position. My **adrenaline** flowed as I ran and dodged through the jungle. Halfway there I slowed down and crept my way to the fallen man. I crawled farther to the right and slowly came up on the side. I could hear a Vietcong talking and a man breathing heavily. I worked my way closer, pulled the **vegetation** away, and saw a Vietcong soldier. He had a pistol pushed against the forehead of Ed Morales. Ed had already been shot in the chest, and there was blood everywhere. I looked around, but I could see no one else. I rose slowly from the bush and set my gun on the Vietcong. He glanced over and saw me. We stared at each other for what seemed like an eternity. The sweat ran down his face, and I could see the hatred in his black eyes. He jerked the pistol from Ed and swung it toward me. I shot him, and he tumbled to the jungle floor. "Have mercy on me, God," I whispered.

I picked up Ed and carried him in my arms in front of me. He was still alive. I tracked back the way I came as fast as I could. I must have just missed the land mine on the way over to get Ed, but this time I stepped right on top of it. I remember hearing the explosion and flying through the air in extreme pain. Then I passed out into the blackness and screamed.

The next memory I have is a beautiful nurse smiling down at me. She reached down and wiped the sweat off my forehead. Betty had been to my bedside as much as she possibly could. My life was on the line from all the blood loss. For days I had been going in and out of consciousness. Once, when Betty turned to

> get a dry towel, I grabbed her arm. It startled her, but she did not push away.
>
> We gazed at each other, and I finally asked, "Are you an angel?" Suddenly, my grip went weak and my eyes slowly closed. They told me it was six days before I opened my eyes. Again, Betty was at my side.

Joel Simpson pulls a Kleenex from his pocket and wipes the tears from his eyes. Then he looks at his grandson Chad.

"That angel was your grandmother. After we both got out of the Army, we got married and moved to Kentucky to be near her family. And she has been with me ever since. She is my best friend." Betty walks over and kisses the old man on the cheek. Joel tells Chad there was one more thing he wanted to tell him. Then the story would be over.

"They told me in the hospital that Ed Morales died instantly from the explosion. His body absorbed a lot of the blast, and that's why I'm alive today. We fought together, and he was my friend." The old man gazes out the window.

Chad looks at the wheelchair and at the spot where there should be legs, but there were no legs. "Grandpa, were you mad at God when you lost your legs and couldn't run anymore?"

Joel thinks for a couple of seconds. "At first I was mad at God. But I came to realize that God was my Shepherd who had led me through the valley of the shadow of death. I know in my heart that I will run in the fields of Heaven with His Son Jesus." A smile shines on the face of the old man. Chad walks over and hugs his grandfather and tells him how much he loves him. He looks down and sees the sticker on his grandpa's wheelchair. He has seen it before, but at this point, he understands. It reads, "Wheels."

That night Joel and Betty go to bed. There will be no fighting the enemy tonight. The old man falls asleep. He sleeps in peace.

VIETNAM SOLDIERS

They fought in a war
And in a place they did not understand.
They fought for the country
And the people they believed in.
They fought with pride
And they fought with fear.
Many died
And many were wounded.
Some are still fighting the war.

Vocabulary

bayonets: weapons like daggers made to fit on the ends of rifles

draft: a picking of persons for required military service

education deferment: an allowance by the government for one to avoid military service because of college enrollment

basic training: the first part of training for a military recruit

compound: an enclosed area containing a group of buildings

recruits: a newly enlisted or drafted member of the armed forces

ethnic: relating to groups of people with common cultural backgrounds

fatigues: standard military clothing

infantry school: the place where new recruits are trained to be foot soldiers

essential: very important

combat: active fighting in war

battalion: a large body of troops

platoon sergeant: an officer in the army with a rank just below that of first sergeant

plateaus: a flat area of high land

ruck sacks: packs similar to backpacks with two adjustable padded shoulder straps and intended to be worn on the back.

hover: to hang fluttering in the air

land mines: an explosive device placed in the ground or water and set to explode when disturbed

callous: being hardened and thickened

Vietcong: a soldier in the Vietnamese Communist movement

adrenaline: a hormone that increases the speed of the heart and raises blood pressure

vegetation: plant life

Comprehension Questions

1. How did Joel feel about getting drafted? Give evidence for your answer.
2. What kind of military training did Joel have to go through before being sent to Vietnam?
3. When Mike Barnett was rude to Joel during the Bible study, how did Joel respond? What can we learn from this?
4. How did Ed Morales involuntarily save Joel's life?
5. How did Joel's faith help him during his time in Vietnam? How did Joel's faith help him put his injury in perspective?

Extension Activity

What are your thoughts and feelings about a military draft? Would you be in favor of having the draft reinstated? Write a paragraph sharing your thoughts.

Sources and Permissions

Unit 1: American Tales

Carolyn Sherwin Bailey

For the Children's Hour. Springfield, MA: Milton Bradley Co., 1906.

Johnny Appleseed: The Life of John Chapman (*originally entitled* Apple-Seed John)

James MacGillivray

Originally published in the *Detroit News,* July 24, 1910.

Round River (*originally* The Round River Drive)

L. Frank Baum

American Fairy Tales. Chicago: George M. Hill, 1901.

The Girl Who Owned a Bear

The Wonderful Pump

Unit 2: Davy Crockett

Davy Crockett

A Narrative of the Life of David Crockett of the State of Tennessee. Philadelphia: E. L. Carey and A. Hart, 1834, pp. 174–194.

Excerpts from "Bear Hunting in Tennessee"

Lawton B. Evans

With Pack and Saddle. Springfield, MA: Milton Bradley Co., 1930.

Be Sure You're Right, Then Go Ahead

S. E. Schlosser

Used with permission from S. E. Schlosser and <http://americanfolklore.net/>.

Sally Ann Thunder Ann Whirlwind Crockett Bests Mike Fink

Unit 3: The War of 1812

Mara Pratt

American History Stories: Vol. III. Boston: Educational Publishing Co., 1890.

The War of 1812

Lawton B. Evans

America First. Springfield, MA: Milton Bradley Co., 1920.

Old Ironsides

Francis Scott Key

First published as "Defense of Fort McHenry" in 1814 and became the national anthem by an act of Congress in 1931.

The Star-Spangled Banner

Unit 4: Westward Ho!

Lawton B. Evans

With Pack and Saddle. Springfield, MA: Milton Bradley Co., 1930.

The Old Miner's Story
What Ben Did to a Bear
The Redwood Tells Its Story

Unit 5: The Civil War

Gertrude van Duyn Southworth

Builders of Our Country, Volume II. New York: D. Appleton & Co., 1907.

Clara Barton

Lawton B. Evans

America First. Springfield, MA: Milton Bradley Co., 1920.

Abraham Lincoln
The Surrender of General Lee

Mara L. Pratt

American History Stories: Vol. IV. Boston: Educational Publishing Co., 1891.

Eddy the Drummer Boy

Francis Miles Finch

The Blue and the Gray and Other Verses. New York: Henry Holt and Co., 1909.

The Blue and the Gray

Unit 6: Important People: Turn of the Century

Patsy Stevens

Taken from *The Booker T. Washington Papers*. Urbana & Chicago: University of Illinois Press, 1972 (Washington's writings span fifty-five years, 1860–1915).

Booker T. Washington

Oliver Otis Howard

First published in 1908. Taken from *Famous Indian Chiefs I have Known*. New York: The Century Co., 1916.

The Great War Chief Joseph of the Nez Percés

Julia H. Johnston

Fifty Missionary Heroes Every Boy and Girl Should Know. New York: Fleming H. Revell Co., 1913.

Dr. Eleanor Chestnut: Missionary Martyr of Lien Chou China
Adoniram Judson: Missionary to Burma

Unit 7: The Life of the Cowboy

Lawton B. Evans

America First. Springfield, MA: Milton Bradley Co., 1920.

The Cowboy

Christopher Scott

Downloaded with permission from <http://www.ropeandwire.com/index.html>.

The Last Ride

Tom Sheehan

Downloaded with permission from <http://www.ropeandwire.com/index.html>.

If There Ever Was a Pair

L. Frank Baum

American Fairy Tales. Chicago: George M. Hill, 1901.

The Capture of Father Time

Unit 8: Tales of the Rails

Adapted by Elizabeth Kearney

Content gathered from the following websites:

<http://www.ibiblio.org/john_henry/>

<http://americanfolklore.net/folklore/2010/07/john_henry.html>

<http://www.voanews.com/learningenglish/home/a-23-2006-06-05-voa1-83130867.html>

<http://www.rofilms.com/page62.htm>

John Henry: A Steel Driving Wonder

W. T. Blankenship

The earliest *John Henry* stories were known as "hammer songs" but over time developed into ballads; the current version was probably published circa 1900.

John Henry, Steel Driving Man

James Baldwin

An American Book of Golden Deeds. New York: American Book Co., 1907.

Thomas Hovenden

Wallace Saunders

Attributed to Wallace Sauders; adapted by Lawrence Seibert and Edward Newton and called "Casey Jones, The Brave Engineer," published circa 1900.

The Ballad of Casey Jones

Unit 9: The Twentieth Century

Lawton B. Evans

America First. Springfield, MA: Milton Bradley Co., 1920.

The Sinking of the *Lusitania*

Phoebe Amory

Taken from Phoebe Amory's memoir, *The Death of the Lusitania*, 1917.

The Death of the *Lusitania* (poem)

C. Douglas Sterner

Used with permission from C. Douglas Sterner and <HomeOfHeroes.com>.

Cher Ami

Harry Webb Farrington

Poems from France. New York: Rough & Brown Press, 1920.

Cher Ami (poem)

Jennie Clare Adams

Used with permission from Women's American Baptist Foreign Mission Society.

The Hills Shall Not Imprison Me

Wayne Roe

Used with permission from Wayne Roe.

Wheels